Talent
for
Humanity

Stories of Creativity, Compassion, and Courage
to Inspire You on Your Journey

Talent
for
Humanity

edited by PATRICK GAFFNEY

GREENLEAF
BOOK GROUP PRESS

Published by Greenleaf Book Group Press
Austin, Texas
www.gbgpress.com

Distributed by Greenleaf Book Group

For ordering information or special discounts for bulk purchases, please contact Greenleaf Book Group at PO Box 91869, Austin, TX 78709, 512.891.6100.

Design and composition by Greenleaf Book Group
Cover design by Greenleaf Book Group
Cover image: ©iStockphoto.com/kotoffei

Cataloging-in-Publication data is available.

ISBN: 978-1-62634-181-4

Part of the Tree Neutral* program, which offsets the number of trees consumed in the production and printing of this book by taking proactive steps, such as planting trees in direct proportion to the number of trees used: www.treeneutral.com

Printed in the United States of America on acid-free paper

TreeNeutral*

15 16 17 18 19 20   10 9 8 7 6 5 4 3 2 1

First Edition

Dedicated to Dominique Lapierre
and all who are striving
to make this world a better place

Contents

FOREWORD

I am convinced that each and every one of us can achieve
something by using our talent—whatever it may be—to help
make this world into the kind of place we dream of living in.

We are all born with the power to imagine what does not yet exist.
What if we used this power to create that very world we all dream of
living in—for ourselves and for others?

Seven portraits appear in this book: seven lives, seven passions,
seven vivid examples of the capacity we all have to change this world
of ours. Ever since I first met the men and women who tell their stories
here, I have been struck by the way they are each using their imagination and creativity to help shape a world that is different, one that
reflects the very best qualities of the human spirit. I mean qualities
like love, generosity, respect, compassion, tolerance, and harmony.
As I got to know these seven people better, I came to understand that

they had all struggled with injustice, hardship, or misery of different kinds and had not only overcome them but transformed them as well. They had grasped the rage, frustration, or helplessness that we all experience at one time or another and, instead of being alienated or paralyzed, converted those feelings into action, and so brought real and lasting benefit to many, many people.

How did they do this? They took their own individual skills, talents, and interests and decided to place them at the service of other human beings. They created what you could call a beautiful fusion of passion and compassion, as miraculous as it was daring. By so doing, they found their own lives infused with meaning, and at the same time they handed us all a powerful invitation: to find our own hidden talents and help create a fairer and more merciful world. "Wouldn't it be wonderful," I thought, "to share their stories so that other people could be inspired to follow in their footsteps?" Because deep down, aren't we all like them? Don't we all have that same power to create—to imagine something that doesn't yet exist?

That's why I asked these individuals to write their stories down, for people like you and me. And that's the whole purpose of this book: to celebrate these magical, enthralling, and pragmatic lives, and to inspire us to start or continue on our own journey. Then I too was asked to tell my own story and say a little bit about *Talent for Humanity*, about which you will be hearing more. So I had to go back in my mind more than forty years and begin to dig up my memories of growing up as a teenager in France.

• • •

When I was at school in Paris and classes were over for the day, we would always get together in the Place d'Italie at the Café de France. It was a place where our imaginations would run wild, with all our dreams of freedom and justice. Every evening, through a fog of cigarette smoke, we would invent a world of peace where human beings all marched hand in hand. Our youthful enthusiasm had no truck with compromise of any kind, money was never a consideration—a professional career even less so—and our heads were crammed with the names of the exotic places we swore we'd visit when we got older. For us, it was a time when nothing seemed impossible, and we only had to believe in order to see.

In my final year at high school, I was suddenly faced with an unexpected choice: to quit my education altogether as an act of solidarity with a bunch of classmates who had been unjustly expelled, or to stay and put up with the injustice. I chose the former. And so there I was, eighteen years old, on the loose in the world of work and looking for a job, which I found quite soon. I had been trained as an accountant, and I must confess that I was pretty good at it. But still my nights were taken up by dreams of travel, and my passion for wildlife pulled me toward every continent on earth.

Then, one morning I received a bitter reminder of reality, in the form of an official letter from the Department of the Army. It was the call-up for military service, and I was ordered to report to the infantry regiment that I had been assigned to in eastern France, to train as a noncommissioned officer cadet. Apart from tearing myself away from the love of my family and leaving my fiancée behind, I was going to have to make an enormous compromise and accept to carry a weapon that had been designed to kill. The army embodied the complete opposite of all my cherished ideals of nonviolence. It was going to mean betraying utterly those men and women whose example I was trying, in my own humble way, to follow and who remain the greatest inspirations for my life—figures like Steve Biko, Dr. Martin Luther King Jr., Mahatma Gandhi, His Holiness the Dalai Lama, Rosa Parks, and Maya Angelou.

It was in the barracks, which came straight out of a novel by Kafka, that I pulled off my very first gesture of protest, the kind of thing that was going to typify the beginning of my adult life. One day at rifle inspection, instead of placing my gun in the hands of the staff sergeant, I flung it onto the ground. Three months of bullying followed before I got a discharge.

Back in civilian life and now nearly twenty, I found myself on the verge of a life that was light-years away from the one I had dreamed of in the Café de France. Admittedly, there were a few foreign trips in the pipeline, but a life of sheer relentless monotony seemed all that stretched out ahead of me. I began to sink into a serious depression, asking myself the same questions over and over again: Why was I here on earth? Didn't every human being have some part to play? Did God exist? They're the kind of questions that stay unanswered because they lie buried in the depths of our souls.

One evening, at the end of a very drunken dinner with some friends, I took a bet that would change my life. On one of the walls of the apartment was a map of the world. Next to it there was a dartboard. I announced that I would throw a dart at the map, and wherever it landed, I would go there and stay for several months. It was 1977, and I was twenty-four. It was a time when a lot of young French people were going to Scandinavia for a few months of fun. So I took aim at northern Europe. The alcohol didn't help, though. The dart landed in the north all right, but in the north of Canada, plumb in the middle of Banks Island, an island within the Arctic Circle. That night, I didn't sleep a wink. Was this really the opening I had been waiting for all this time?

For the whole of the next year, with the support and love of my parents, I set about turning the impossible into a reality by organizing an expedition to the Arctic. Thanks to a whole group of generous sponsors, in June 1978 my fiancée, two friends, and I took off for a year of adventures in the remotest places on the planet. We were going to travel across the Arctic from west to east, sleeping in tents and igloos. For me, this was an extraordinary experience, and for many reasons. For a start, it represented my very first "corporate development plan." Convincing a multitude of partners to back us was a revelation in itself, because it summoned up talents that until then I had no inkling I possessed. Then, there was my encounter with the Inuit people, which came as a complete eye-opener into what is meant by "knowledge," because where they live everything I had learned at school proved to be almost devoid of any meaning. Finally, my dream of discovering different species of wildlife in their natural setting at last came true.

By the time I got back to France in July 1979, I had made a promise to myself that I was going to live out this passion of mine for discovering the world and meeting people from different cultures. However, in 1981, while I was preparing for a trip to Baffin Island, another choice came up. I joined a concert production company, not realizing that my life was going to take another new twist, and this time it was going to lure me into spending eighteen years making decisions that were basically about pampering my ego, and which would end up distancing me absolutely from the adult that I had dreamed of becoming when I was remaking the world with my friends in the Café de France.

• • •

More and more depressed and less and less able to control my mood swings, I was becoming hard to live with for those around me, and at the beginning of 1999 I decided to leave for Nepal with my eleven-year-old daughter. I wanted to connect with life and people again, get to know my daughter, and find out what it was that linked me to other living beings—and to myself. Our guide in Nepal, Karma Sherpa, led me onto a path of simplicity and taught me how to slow down. He helped me see that everyday life offers us miracles that we no longer know how to notice. In short, Karma gave me the courage

I needed to change the whole direction of my life, and he will always be one of my dearest friends.

After I got back from the Himalayas, I ran into some amazing people, and these meetings moved me forward down my path of self-discovery, that painful but incredible journey that draws a human being closer to his or her true nature. It is a journey that is nothing like a "career" and yet totally about ourselves all the same. What I slowly came to discover was that if we manage to love and be at peace with ourselves, then it's as if a new day dawns, not just for us, but for the entire world as well. The impact that one person's transformation can have on others is extraordinary. And it was this fascination for the power of transformation that led me to create *Talent for Humanity*. But this is not solely my creation or that of my friends. It is yours too. Because I believe that *we* can transform the world, each and every one of us, and the first move is our own. There is no perfect moment for starting out on this path. No best age, either. And it is never, never too late.

The women and men we are introducing you to in this book are just like you and me. It's simply that one day they decided to follow the path that they took because they were inspired by others or touched by a meeting that transformed their lives. Some of them started out on their journey not so long ago, while others have already gone some way down the road and changed the lives of hundreds, even millions, of people—although the numbers are not so important.

I would like to dedicate this book to Dominique Lapierre. He is an example of the truth that every human being possesses the power to transform the world. His talent as a writer and the subjects he writes about in his books have been an enormous inspiration for me in shaping *Talent for Humanity*. This man offered his talent and his creativity to the world, and because of that talent he transformed the lives of millions.

I hope the individuals whose stories we have related here will inspire you and move you too. Actually, the final chapter of this book belongs to you. The blank pages that accompany it are offered to you, to open your heart to humanity. In fact, your *Letter to Humanity* is the beginning of our communal story. Do join us and take part. For I am convinced that each and every one of us can achieve something by using our talent—whatever it may be—to help make this world into the kind of place we dream of living in.

Even if we are but tiny individual drops of water, together we can make a stream, a river, or a sea. You know, I believe we *are* all like drops of water. Somewhere we dream of merging one day into a sea of wisdom. We are born in clear springs, rush downstream as torrents—unrestrained, wild, and turbulent—and then blend into the calm of the river as it winds its way downward toward the vast expanse of the ocean into which we dream of melting. Some will live this adventure in its entirety, others will evaporate and reappear in that clear spring that gives birth to everything that lives. One single thing is common to us all, women and men alike, and that is the impossibility of swimming against the stream of life.

Have I found the answers to those questions that harried me in my youth? One thing I have realized is that the greatest gift I ever received was the love my parents gave me. Love is such a powerful remedy for troubles of the soul and the heart. If ever anyone asked my advice I would tell them, "Don't ever hold back, I implore you, from giving your love." And so yes, today I have found the answers to some of those questions. What's more, I have made up my mind about one thing: I aim to die with a smile on my face, because I don't want a single regret when it is my turn to evaporate.

Every night now, it seems, I find myself back at the Café de France. Except that it is no longer just a dream; it is my life.

Please don't forget: the world has need of you.

Thierry Sanchez
For *Talent for Humanity*

INTRODUCTION

We all know this so well. It happens every day, whenever we look someone in the face and there is that electric meeting of the eyes. A bolt of recognition spins out and bounds across, and in a split second a whole universe of possibilities opens up. "Remember me," those eyes seem to whisper, "remember I am yearning to find meaning, just like you; aching to be happy, just like you; struggling to fend off trouble and suffering, just like you."

There are seven billion, in fact, just like us, and perhaps ten billion by the end of the century. We are surrounded by others all the time, and one of the inescapable truths of our human reality is that although we are each unique, we are all ultimately the same, with the same secret fears and aspirations, the same tendency to make mistakes, the same need for connection and friendship, and the same capacity to find out what on earth our life is all about.

Another truth, one that becomes more obvious every day, is that we are all intimately and intricately interconnected. We depend on others for absolutely everything we use, consume, or enjoy, and even our very attitudes of mind, our words, and our actions constantly weave us into relating with others. Whether it's our mother, brothers, sisters, children, or the person who delivers the mail or fills the shelves at the supermarket, the list of people we depend on for our survival is actually endless. We live in a teeming sea of tiny acts of cooperation and kindness, where it's impossible to untangle our well-being from that of others.

And yet we live in a world that is deeply fractured, where it's harder and harder to show each other affection, and where the underlying belief is the idea of the separateness of "us" and "them." So it's a world fraught with injustice, inequality, oppression, cruelty, and misery, as well as everyday pain and panic and anxiety. Even those of us who do not live in the shadow of warfare and conflict, or the pain of illness, will suffer from depression or loneliness or will struggle to find connection and meaning.

All of us dream of a kinder world, a more equal world, a more inclusive and imaginative world where our common vision somehow matches the vast and mysterious beauty of being human. How often do we stop to consider a simple question like, "What does it mean to be alive as a human being?" And in this very brief time we have here on earth, have we calculated what we are going to do with this life of ours? We might wonder how we are going to choose to behave and act in our community and contribute to an endangered world, or ask ourselves what we understand by the word "responsibility." We may tell ourselves we desperately want to do something to help. Will we just settle for business as usual, though, merely following the unconscious, automatic, ravenous bidding of "my needs" and "my feelings"? What part are we going to play?

The six stories in this book trace the lives and actions of a group of people who have found answers to these questions and made an incredible contribution to their fellow human beings. In one way or another, they have all taken a stand and fought against poverty, apathy, closed-mindedness, oppression, and prejudice. Their stories range from revolutionary Iran to Skid Row in Los Angeles, from a Native American reservation in Montana to Norway and Great Britain, from Palestine and Israel to the slums of Calcutta and the Sochi Olympics. They embrace the entire planet.

What is it that brings this particular group of women and men together? Some years ago, Thierry Sanchez, an enterprising Frenchman with wide experience in the world of art, music, and concert production, was prompted by his experiences and meetings with remarkable people to found a charity called *Talent for Humanity*. Along with many of his friends—artists, businesspeople, and everyday citizens—he envisioned an organization that would celebrate the work of some of the women and men in different parts of the world who are giving of themselves to help and support others. These are individuals who may be unknown outside of their own communities but who quite simply change the world every day. The task of *Talent for Humanity* is to shine a light on people who have harnessed their passion, their gifts, and their creativity to a desire to serve others. Out of this came the idea of the Human Spirit Award. The individuals chosen for this award would not be handed a statue or a plaque, but their stories and their mission in life would be recounted in a book, the one you are holding right now. The seven individuals featured in these pages are the first to be offered this award as a tribute to their passion, their unswerving determination, and their vision as they strive to improve the destiny and lives of others. And the aim of this book is to plant the seeds of their inspiration in the hearts of anyone who comes across it.

Each of our storytellers here was invited to compose a *Letter to Humanity*, which follows immediately after their story. In their letters, they crystallize what they would like to say, from their hearts, to all of us in the world. At the end of this book you will find an invitation where you too can write your own letter and express your deepest or most urgent feelings to people everywhere. In that way, we may all gradually become part of an openhearted community of people who are passionate about transforming the world, each in our own different way.

One deep source of inspiration for Thierry and his colleagues has been the work of Dominique Lapierre, the author of many books, including the heartrending *City of Joy*. Here is someone who has used his flair as a journalist and writer to help thousands through the charitable foundations and humanitarian projects he has launched.

His message is, in his own words, that "we can all make this world a better, a juster world by extending a fraternal hand to the poor, the destitute, the homeless, the unwanted, the unloved." And as we wonder how we, of all people, could change the world, so this book is offered to help give us that extra ounce of courage, to push open the door and start our own journey, whatever that might be.

Let us briefly introduce the individuals featured in this book. We begin with **Reza**, who collided with his own mission in life during the chaotic days and nights of the Iranian Revolution. He tells his story with all the lingering grace and magic of Persian culture. Living now in exile in France, he has become a legendary photojournalist and a prolific campaigner for children and people in need, whose work in Afghanistan and other countries around the world, offering trainings for example in media and communication, has earned him many honors and awards, including France's Légion d'Honneur. For years he has focused on regions devastated by war and conflict, in the knowledge that his photos could awaken understanding and therefore provoke change. Reza founded the NGO "Aina," and he continues to mount exhibitions and offer workshops all over the planet.

On the far side of the world in Los Angeles, **Sherry and Bob Jason**, husband and wife attorneys who work as public defenders, were so horrified by the plight of at-risk inner city children in impoverished and underserved neighborhoods plagued by drugs, gangs, and crime that they created "City Hearts," an innovative and revolutionary program that trains young people in the arts, allowing them to discover their own potential, find a vision of a brighter future, and so become caring and creative participants in the community. Bob and Sherry staked everything they had on City Hearts, with remarkable results. In the past thirty years, they have trained and transformed the lives of 35,000 children and young people with this extraordinary program.

Aliza Hava is a peacemaker. A gifted and dedicated singer and songwriter born in America, her lifelong passion for music coincided with a profound spiritual awakening, which guided her toward a vision of organizing concerts for peace. Based in Israel for a number of years, she worked toward creating tolerance, understanding, and peaceful coexistence among the different communities in the Middle East, making use of the healing power of music. She created huge events such as Peace Day LIVE, which involved nine concerts on six continents, and the largest-ever interfaith prayer festival and concert Harmony in the Holy Land, which gathered together Muslims, Christians, and Jews and was streamed to countries all over the world. Aliza currently lives in California.

It was music that also shaped the life of **Deeyah**, who was born in Norway to Pakistani and Afghan parents and trained in the traditional South Asian style of music and singing. While still young, she became a well-known pop singer, incurring the wrath of the conservative members of her ethnic community who sought to silence her. Fleeing to the United Kingdom and then the United States, she was drawn to helping the marginalized and oppressed and those denied a voice or freedom, and she went on to discover a deep and unflinching commitment to human rights and social activism. In particular Deeyah has drawn attention to the scourge of so-called honor killings, winning the International Emmy Award for Best Current Affairs Film in 2013 for her documentary about honor killings in the UK entitled *Banaz: A Love Story*. Deeyah continues to create music as a talented producer and composer.

Born in the United States, **Yarrow Kraner** was destined to become a gardener of genius. His baptism by fire on a Native American reservation in Montana reinforced his innate aptitude for connecting people to a common purpose and initiated him into the power of tolerance and forgiveness. Yarrow's gift for recognizing the extraordinary in everyday people led him to found "Superdudes," an original online community for serving the community all over America. This then evolved into "HATCH," a unique mentoring environment where thousands of young people have found their lives transformed through working with experts in a dazzling variety of disciplines and professions, including filmmakers, musicians, photographers, designers, architects, writers, fine artists, and specialists in the entertainment industry.

Finally, **Daniele Finzi Pasca** is a theater director and clown who grew up in the Italian-speaking part of Switzerland and traveled to India to serve the sick and the dying in Mother Teresa's centers in Calcutta. Returning to Europe, he founded the "Theatre of Caress" and now has a worldwide reputation as a deeply creative and revolutionary stage director, responsible for the closing ceremony of the Winter Olympics and opening of the Paralympics in Sochi in 2014.

In his creations, he is possessed by a desire to evoke compassion and humanity in his spectators by teasing out the human condition with all its joy, inspiration, pathos, paradox, and humor. In an exuberant and kaleidoscopic stream of consciousness quite different from the other narratives, Daniele's story is interspersed with ideas, visions, and techniques that figure in his love affair with his many audiences around the world.

These six stories are all wildly different, some of them poetic, others more down-to-earth, but what they all have in common is the way in which these men and women have uncovered something within themselves that empowered them to help and create opportunities for others, often on a massive and until then unthinkable scale. They all have used the arts, whether film, theater, photography, drama, dance, or music, and allowed their gifts and talents to reach out and infuse others, often young people and children, with values and understanding that are vital for their future and the community.

As they tell their stories in their own words, it will become clear that this book is neither another self-help book nor a set of moral directives about what anyone is supposed to think, believe, or put into action. Far from it. This is a book about passion and creativity, about friendship and kindness, determination and, as we will see, focused and undistracted attention. It is a book about compassion, because everyone in it has been driven by a compelling desire to alleviate suffering, along with its causes. It is a book about courage and resilience as well, as they all in their own ways had to overcome obstacles and hardships and sometimes the most grueling and brutal of ordeals. It is about transformation, too. Some people like to make a distinction between change and transformation. They say that change is an improvement or alteration of what already exists, while transformation, like a butterfly freeing itself from the chrysalis, means a new creation where the only limits are our imagination and commitment.

As you will see, none of these men and women set out to be catalysts for change in the world or the source of hope and help for so many other people. It so happened that each of them possessed a deep affinity with art and creativity, whether in the form of music, dance, networking, photography, or theater. All of them had significant artistic talents. But what transpires as we follow them through the formative years of their lives is that they each experienced a dramatic moment of transformation and so came to realize that those very gifts required, demanded almost, that they apply them to the service of humanity, whether to help children or women or ordinary people in Afghanistan, the United Kingdom, or Palestine. There was a point where they could no longer bear the suffering of others, and to the same extent they could not stand the thought of inaction. In this sense, they all fought against convention, against the communal delusion that we are separate and independent entities. They all possessed the courage to be different and so make a difference, shining a light through the fog of normality, a light made all the brighter because it had its source in the heart of humanity, the living flame of love. And so this is a book about love as well, about connection and the wish to bring the greatest possible well-being and freedom to others.

When ten more children in Los Angeles at risk from the revolving door of gang warfare and juvenile crime find their way to a better, more hopeful life, bringing the best of themselves to the community, or when one young woman finds the hand of friendship without being murdered for simply seeking freedom and the right to choose her own life, then we can see how the impact of these people, each working in their own way, is exponential, affecting the lives of innumerable other human beings in an ever-widening cascading torrent of interconnections.

The themes and the insights in this book are a formula for our world today, a message for us all; in fact nothing could be more relevant or more urgent. These stories are intensely personal and profoundly universal. They are about humanity, in both senses of the word, from the collective, our species, to those essential and most noble qualities of the human heart: kindness and benevolence, altruism and love.

This is also a book of discovery, and as we read we might find it is full of clues and insights and ideas that might strike and move through our minds like a rush of mountain air. But that is up to us as we meet and make eye contact with the women and men in these pages. They are human beings just like us. And to be a human being is to be creative. We all have the capacity to transform ourselves, change the world, and inspire others.

What did our storytellers find on their journeys? Definitely they have encountered the great paradoxical and counterintuitive truth of the human condition, that taking care of other human beings is the surest and most reliable way of take caring of our self. Because for all their gifts and abilities, what they, and we, discover is that these seven individuals had one more talent, perhaps the most precious and far-reaching one of all—a talent for humanity.

My Seven Voyages

by R E Z A

I have a dream that all human beings, each and every
one, will play an active part in the evolution of humanity.
Let's all take action . . . let's each dream of a seed, one that
grows into a vast tree of peace.

As far back as I can remember, afternoons in my childhood were
marked by a kind of ritual, a mystery that was only finally solved
once I learned how to read. In the afternoon, my father, who worked
as a simple civil servant, would shut himself away in a room with a
Persian carpet and comfortable cushions on the floor. My mother
used to wait for him to come home, heating up the samovar with
its red-hot embers, on which would sit the teapot, in pride of place.
On the ground lay a tray decked out with little bowls full of dried
fruits and pistachio nuts. A number of men, friends of my father's,
would closet themselves away with him. All through their afternoon

rest time, there prevailed a respectful and healing silence which we were not allowed to disrupt, even in the slightest. So as soon as the first days of fine weather arrived, we would attempt to take over the garden and its pool with our games.

Some time after I had begun school and the cryptic letters were beginning to make sense, my father solemnly yet tenderly announced that I could come inside the forbidden room, but to do nothing except watch and listen. And this is how a totally unsuspected world was opened up to me, a world where poets, intellectuals, and men who were just very knowledgeable gathered together to read poetry and spend hours in a sort of informal literary salon, a far cry from any run-of-the mill bourgeois recital. Every now and then, Shahryar, the great poet, used to come by. To me fell the huge privilege of witnessing their discussions firsthand and, later on, of occasionally reading aloud the texts they had selected.

This was the first of my voyages, into the world of words and poetry, which have left such a deep and lasting impression on Persian culture.

• • •

By the start of my teenage years, I was a serious student, and I had just left Tabriz, the town where I was born, to live with relatives in Tehran. The college in which my father had enrolled me was the best in the city. Even so, despite my exam results, which put me way ahead near the top of the class, and despite the various national math and chess competitions that I managed to win, I was the object of all the usual jeering that people from the capital heap upon provincials. My broad Tabriz accent was the cause of my woes, and without a doubt this all triggered in me a reckless urge to change the whole way things were going.

One other reason drove me toward becoming inventive. I had to quench my insatiable thirst for reading, which my father's modest salary was unable to afford. I had discovered a disused room on the mezzanine floor of the college, and I had the idea that it could recapture its heart and soul in the form of a library. I shared my plan with my father, who encouraged me, saying his only wish was that I should take complete responsibility for it myself. I can still picture the incredulous, suspicious even, face of the head of the college when I took him through the strategy I had thought up for collecting books for the library. Instantly he summoned my father, to make sure that my initiative was a serious one. He was so reassured by their meeting that he ended up giving me his blessing.

After launching an appeal for gifts of books and magazines to all the parents of the educational institutions in the area, after devoting my holidays to labeling and classifying some 630 books we had collected, and after cleaning the room and putting up shelves, the great day arrived—the inauguration in front of an audience of parents, teachers, and principals, along with some of the students. The official speeches were being given, one after another, when all of a sudden, as if in a dream or rather a nightmare, I heard someone announcing my first name and my family name, and then the school principal inviting me to say a few words. It took a superhuman effort, but I perked up and, still with a tinge of that Tabriz accent, I spoke for a little while. Yet all along, I had never been seeking revenge on my sneering fellow students or recognition from my father, which I already possessed anyway in the serene trust he had shown in me. All I had been looking for was to change the course of history—my own.

The following summer, and every afternoon when classes were over, the library, with me in charge of loans, became my home port, which I would sail away from every time I read something. It was my refuge, for my second voyage.

. . .

In the south of Iran on the Persian Gulf, there is a town called Bandar Abbas, where my father had decided to go into voluntary exile in order to earn himself a bit more money. Civil servants received a bonus if they opted to work in this town with its scorching heat, situated between the desert and the sea. I went with him, while my mother, my sisters, and my brothers all stayed in Tehran. I was sixteen years old at the very most. In Bandar Abbas, the searing heat of the sun was written all over the people's dark brown faces, so different from the faces I had known up until then.

About two years earlier I had discovered photography, thanks to my uncle who had given me a camera. I would often walk around, scanning things with my eyes, and then try to capture what I saw in a few photos, but always sparingly so as to save on film, which was as precious as it was costly.

One morning, all curious and innocent, I decided to go to the fish market. The stalls were overflowing with the catch of the day, and men were haranguing their customers whose eyes were weighing up the produce, on the lookout for a bargain. The smell was so strong it made my head swim and left me feeling quite sick. For several hours on end I strolled about, exploring a world I had been quite unaware of up until then. Suddenly I noticed a hunched figure sitting on the bare earth wrapped in a length of black cloth covered in dust from the ground. In front of her—it turned out to be an old woman—were laid out a few scrawny fish, which had already started rotting after several hours out in the sun.

For a long time I studied this poor, miserable woman in all her distress. For reasons that I could not fathom in my teenage innocence, her family had abandoned her, so vulnerable now in her old age. I took a photo of her, and she called me over. I crouched down close beside her, a little bit afraid and slightly ashamed at having possibly seemed intrusive with my camera. Very quietly, in a voice wracked by age, poverty, and fear, she told me this story: "See here, little one, these few fish, I pick them up off the ground when the fishermen drop them in their haste. They are nothing to look at, but sometimes I manage to get a few pennies for them from people even poorer than me who are happy to have them. But see, that policemen watching us over there won't even let me be here unless I pay him half my earnings."

I came back from that morning's walk a different person, changed forever. Suddenly I had grasped the full meaning of the word "injustice." That sense of outrage and rebellion, which would only go on and on growing inside of me, would end up shaping the entire course of my life.

I had to write this story down, to cry out to the whole world and appeal to those in power. So, I put together a newspaper and distributed it all around my high school. And so was born *Parvaz*, which means "to fly" or "to soar." One day when we were in class, not long after these four pages were published, the door swung open and the principal called out my name. He was holding a copy of *Parvaz* in his hand. Convinced that I was going to be on the receiving end of some complimentary feedback, I paced along behind him, mindlessly failing to pick up his uncharacteristic sternness toward me. In his office, there was a policeman waiting. "Are you the author of this paper?" he snapped. Pulling myself up straight, I replied, "Yes, sir," expecting congratulations, which seemed curiously slow in coming. Straightaway, he ripped apart the pages he was clutching in his hands and flung them in my face, shouting: "Don't ever try that again! Ever! Do you understand?"

When I got home, I told my father the whole story, not really knowing whether I was going to be in for one of his rare fits of rage. But it was quite the opposite, because he declared: "If you think you're doing the right thing, then press on. But just be careful not to get yourself arrested." Two roads were opening up in front of me:

one of inaction and renunciation, and the other, the exposure and denunciation of injustice.

I chose the latter. So the road of fighting for justice and freedom, one littered with pitfalls and dangers, became the path I took on my third voyage.

• • •

As a young student at the School of Fine Arts in the University of Tehran, I divided my free time between taking photos of the world around me and working on the creation of detailed models for a firm of architects in order to fund my studies. At twenty years old, I was looking very intently at the poverty that was such a contrast to the obscene sumptuousness of the life of the Shah and his slavish, fawning, and self-serving court. The people suffered in silence, while the Pahlavi dynasty trumpeted the 2,500 years of the monarchy at Persepolis.

Deep within me, the feeling of protest and rebellion kept stirring and became more compelling as each day went by. I expressed it through my pictures, which showed the conditions of the common people, pictures that I stuck up extremely carefully in secret at night on the walls of the city, like tiny traces of truth denouncing the monstrous farce in which we all were living.

One summer's evening, the day after my birthday, which adults in the East do not observe but leave to children to celebrate, I was engrossed in finishing off a model with the help of some friends in our workshop. The dry, oppressive heat had engulfed our night's work, but we didn't really care, as we were happy to be together, in all the thrill of our twenties and exhilarated by our unshakeable conviction that the world was just waiting for the changes that we, of course, were going to supply.

Already Tehran had become a capital city that was expanding as if, as each day went by, it was less and less able to contain its booming population. Many of the houses and the occasional small apartment building had flat roofs, where whole families, fleeing the suffocating heat indoors, would go to sleep on mattresses, seeking a chance puff of wind and the hoped-for coolness of the morning dew that would come every day at dawn with the muezzin's call to prayer.

That night, a sharp, violent hammering on the door cut through our student chatter. Standing there were a number of armed, plain-clothes policemen, who, we discovered, belonged to the Shah's secret police. We each got up and identified ourselves. When I uttered my name, their tone of voice turned noticeably harder. I was the only one to whom they said: "You, follow us. We're going round to your place." Little by little, as we made our way across town, I seemed to drift further and further away from my adolescence. I didn't know why the treatment they had given me was so different from that which they had reserved for my friends. But already I had been singled out as an "other." The silence in the car was crushing. I thought about how frightened my parents were going to feel when they were woken in the middle of the night. My mind flickered between a blank emptiness, numb to what was actually happening, and a deluge of jostling thoughts, memories, and questions.

My parents were roused by the callous, heavy-handed intrusion of the policemen, who loomed on either side of me. They ransacked my room from top to bottom and confiscated the books, the photos, and all the written documents. And then they arrested me. On the doorstep, they blurted out a parting remark to my parents that was supposed to be reassuring: "Don't worry. We've just got a few questions to ask him." As the car started up, I caught sight of my mother and father huddled together, one against the other, as if the whole ordeal had suddenly shrunk them and made them physically smaller.

In the interrogation room at the prison, they questioned me without a break, asking me to betray the names of accomplices that I had never had. My photos represented a kind of social action that was entirely solitary—one of simply bearing witness, on my own. However this was a reality the police would not accept. For five months, they tortured me every day, trying to make me confess that I belonged to some nonexistent political organization. When this was over, my body was given a break, and I was incarcerated for over two and a half years. I found myself at a different kind of university during these years, as I was surrounded by intellectuals, poets, writers, and politicians, all suffering the same fate as me.

Resistance in the name of freedom of conscience, in the horrific Evin Prison, constituted my fourth voyage.

• • •

In Tehran, a sprawling and noisy city, my brother and I shared a house that, on account of its simple, original architecture and its distinctive decoration, became the epicenter for parties and other get-togethers with our friends. My student days and the interlude in prison were behind me, and since then I had worked for an architectural firm. I savored these years, independent as I was and discovering life like any young man who is free. Photography was always my companion on my solitary walks.

In the alleyways of the working-class areas, on the benches in the universities and on the carpets of the mosques, a wind of protest and dissent was springing up against the excesses of a monarchy that thought it could hypnotize the people with the glamour of its gilded lifestyle. Demonstrations against the regime began to multiply, and the repression by the Shah's police force and army turned bloody.

One day, I witnessed it with my own eyes. Some young demonstrators were moving forward, barely restrained by the police. Suddenly, a shot rang out and a young man dropped to the ground, dead. I saw a student with a camera running to capture the scene. For ages, I watched the confrontation, transfixed by the reality of what was happening in front of me.

I took three days off to put myself at the heart of the action and take photos. Rather than stay a passive witness, I finally decided to become an eyewitness photographer and handed back the keys to the architects' office where I was working. It was around this time that the country slid into a revolution unlike anything before it. The whole royal order was overthrown and driven into lifelong exile. I made a point of following each new incident that convulsed the streets and every altercation that pitted the clergy against the left-wing politicians. Overwhelmed by the revolution, the repression, and the violence of the tragic war with Iraq, all coming one on top of the other, Iran went into mourning. I had chosen images—photos—as my way of telling the story.

On the other side of the world, my photographs struck a chord with the international press, while in my homeland, I was definitely beginning to upset the mullahs. They had won power largely with the support of the countries in the West who were now gradually discovering, to their surprise, what the stakes were in this game of manipulation, and that they had been the very first victims. Iran was closing itself off and slowly becoming the land of every provocation, every crime, and every kind of defiance and resistance.

In secret, I traveled to the inaccessible region of Kurdistan to expose the clerical regime's atrocities against the Kurdish people. As I went undercover, I lost my family name and kept Reza as my pen name, in the hope of covering my tracks. Everywhere, the government bombing and shelling had mangled the villages and wreaked havoc on the environment. Men grieved over the betrayals, the summary executions, the wounded, and the dead. After seventeen days, I surfaced with a haul of several thousand photos that were published far and wide. I left again, this time for the front line in the war against Iraq, where I was injured when a piece of shrapnel lodged itself in my hand. Two major events marked the few days when I was back in Tehran: the doctors wanted to amputate my hand to avoid a fatal case of gangrene, and I learned that I was on the blacklist of the next people to be taken into custody, which was a synonym in those days for immediate conviction with no right of appeal. So, on the pretext of a medical emergency, I sidestepped the vigilant scrutiny of the authorities, took my injured hand and a small bag, and left the country on March 21, 1981.

The long road of exile was that of my fifth voyage.

• • •

Lonesome wandering was my way of life for the next eight years. I had chosen Paris as my anchorage, as fragile as it was fleeting. But it could just as well have been New York or Rome; wherever I went, I was just passing through. My favorite places were the zones of war or repression, things that I witnessed firsthand over and over again, as I was often treading the frontier between life and death and dodging the latter thanks to some sixth sense perhaps, or more simply because of destiny, the *maktub* ("it is written") so dear to Middle Eastern culture.

Lebanon, Afghanistan, South Africa, the Philippines, and Pakistan were my other adopted countries, each one as ephemeral as France. My family, who had stayed in Iran, was subjected to yet more horrors: war with its terrors and hardships, and the Islamist regime with its reactionary ideology and repression. I never saw my father again. His heart had been weakened, what with my leaving, my brother's departure a few years later, and the arrests as well, and it finally gave out. I heard of his death on a freezing cold day while patiently waiting for hours for the heads of state to emerge from some international conference in Lausanne where they had sent me "to get a rest from the shelling." It meant that I had to continue traveling down this road of mine without the kindly, loving, indescribable protection of the one who had guided me so much through his quiet trust in my choices. That day I became the head of the family, albeit at a distance. Yet it was a responsibility that I took on more than ever before, regardless of all the roads and borders that separated us.

For a long time, I believed that I would always be alone and that, notwithstanding the sweet, sincere passions that dotted my life as a single man, I would keep the door to love closed and turn my back on a life entangled in relationships.

Paris started to wear on me. It no longer even gave me that sense of refuge required for a home base. Between nostalgia and my chosen duty of eyewitness, I kept trying to make my mark on one part of the history of our times and to leave some unique trace of my presence on earth.

One year, on the first day of summer, musicians invaded the sun-lit streets of the capital. People's faces wore a friendly, smiling look, in striking contrast to the usual mask of drabness, depression, and irritation of city folk in a hurry. Some of them were swaying their hips to the devilish rhythm of improvised jazz music, while others had lost themselves in the feeling of an a cappella vocal that drifted unbidden into the calm of an empty alley. The air was inundated with happiness. I made my way, on my own and a bit exhausted, toward a party that was being held by friends. Meandering along, I captured my moods with my camera, as if I were making notes in some kind of visual logbook. I left the hubbub of the street, stepped through a heavy dark green wooden lodge gate, and walked into an unbelievable paved courtyard where plants awoken by spring were already climbing all over the walls.

And there she was. I was surprised by her solitude; she seemed subtly ill at ease in the middle of this crowd of people all talking to one another, glasses in their hands and smiles on their faces. She stood out slightly on account of her youth, her beauty, the immaculate whiteness of the blouse she was wearing, and the way she surveyed with a watchful and questing gaze what doubtless appeared to her eyes utterly pointless. To me she seemed to be from another world, although she turned out to belong to every world. Our meeting was brief, yet when we shook hands her warm and tender hand held mine for a long time. We exchanged few words but a long gaze—even though she was already making her exit. In that instant, we displayed no feelings. Love made its presence felt without our knowledge, like something inescapable and glaringly obvious.

With love, until now unknown—this is how I began my sixth voyage.

• • •

Because it had acted as the theater for our meeting, Paris now took on anew all the attractions of the city I would call home. Although I was still on the road, still traveling, whether I was overcoming obstacles or winning public recognition, no longer was I the poor wretch all on my own. She was there, and her presence eased my exile and the horror of the fighting I would witness. I longed to tell her about my past, my memories—those things that go to make up a man.

The day my mother breathed out her last exhausted breath, I felt that the sweetness, simplicity, and discreet, constant kindheartedness that had stamped her entire life all rushed back to assault me. Memories of the stories she told me when I was a small child came flooding back, throwing a whole new light on the choices I had made in my life. The "Sinbad" of my childhood was a man who personified all the romantic allure of adventure, poetry, and wisdom. His name was Saadi. He had traveled on foot on the roads of the East for thirty years. Observant by nature, he made a record of his countless rich experiences, which were all so dazzling and exotic in the eyes of a child like me. When he got home, Saadi assembled his writings in two collections of poetry, a source of wisdom in which, scattered here and there, are all the stories that my mother told me. One verse in particular I remember. Years later I was to understand its absolutely universal truth when I found it on a wall at the United Nations in New York:

> *Human beings are all limbs of one body;*
> *All created from the same one essence.*
> *If just one of them suffers, the others cannot rest in peace.*
> *Someone who does not care about the suffering of others*
> *Does not deserve to be called "human."*

This poem, whispered to me so often by my mother, has been reflected back to me on the roads I have traveled, time and time again.

Another tale came back to me that I remember hearing as a child while sitting on a carpet. One day, not far from a stream, an old, old man was planting a walnut tree. Some inconsiderate, bad-mannered kids started sniggering as they were going past and called out: "Hey, grandpa, don't you know that it'll take twenty years before your poor seed becomes a big, strong tree loaded with nuts? In twenty years' time, you won't be around. Don't knock yourself out!" The old man replied, "My dear children, my whole life I have eaten walnuts that grew on trees that had been planted by people other than me before I was even born. I'm planting this one in the ground today so that *your* grandchildren can enjoy the nuts from the tree that is going to grow." When I remembered this, it occurred to me that my whole relationship to time itself, and to the humility we need before the sweep of human history, had been forged, without my ever realizing it, by this little story.

After this period of reliving all these memories about my mother, I needed to feel alive and banish the sadness and nostalgia of her departure. So I went back on the road on my own for a kind of inner exile, which led me into the remote mountains of Badakhshan in Afghanistan. One day, I found myself in a little village forgotten by the mapmakers, still spared from the wars that had ravaged the whole country, when I heard children's voices coming from the gates of a school. I saw a young boy with blond hair and blue eyes. He had about him a profound and almost solemn look, at once sad and yet quite determined. His clothes were too short for him and worn thin by time and poverty. In his hand he was cradling, as if it were some priceless trophy, a new shoot of a plant that he had been growing for a few weeks at school. I asked him: "What are you going to do with that?" Slightly taken aback by my odd question but with a glow of pride, he answered: "I am going to make it into a tree."

Above and beyond the mission to be an eyewitness photographer that I had set myself years before, now my road took on its full meaning and true direction. Commitment to humanitarian action became my seventh voyage.

• • •

"And the others?" you'll ask. What about all the other voyages? Those which happened, which I kept to myself because of forgetfulness or modesty, and those which have not yet been written . . . the eighth . . . and then the ones after that? Well, they are there, among the voyages of those who can dream.

MY LETTER TO HUMANITY

I could have been an architect and turned vacant land into houses, skyscrapers, whole towns, or empires even. But instead I chose something ineffable, something self-evident, something that speaks for itself and that denounces, moves, shocks, and tells a tale without a single word. I chose photography as my language and photojournalism as my duty.

What was my very first tool for creating peace? Photography. That's what got me into telling these not-to-be-forgotten stories of human beings swept up in the turmoil of the world. But above and beyond all the national borders, and despite the cultural differences and the deadly wars, my pictures have never been just one sad account of mangled lives. If they bear witness to anything at all, they tend to show the smile behind the tears, the beauty behind the tragedy, and life as so much stronger than death.

So yes, I could have worked my way to the top in the world of photography, covering the wars, narrating stories with images, and all the while confining myself to my profession—my "reason for living," my role as celebrated photojournalist.

Yes, I could have. But then there's a bigger scale, that of humanity itself, where empires of any kind always turn back into dust. Just so, bearing witness was in fact only one stage in my fight against injustice and for a better world. That's why I had to pick up another staff for my pilgrimage, which was a commitment to concrete action among the living. And ever since, these two—being an eyewitness and serving through taking action—have formed my path through this world, a world that I long to see freed from wars and borders of any kind.

I have a dream that all human beings, each and every one, will play an active part in the evolution of humanity. It makes me think once more of that verse by the Persian poet Saadi:

> Human beings are all limbs of one body;
> All created from the same one essence.
> If just one of them suffers, the others cannot rest in peace.
> Someone who does not care about the suffering of others
> Does not deserve to be called "human."

Today then, let's all take action and do something in solidarity with one another, and let's each dream of a seed, one that grows into a vast tree of peace.

—Reza

Making the World a Better Place Through the Arts

by SHERRY & BOB JASON

What if he had found that piano first,
before he found guns and gangs?

Nine-year-old Eduardo hiked up his blue jeans, strode across the Shakespearean stage at the Will Geer Theatricum Botanicum, and took up his opening position, crouching with his head down. Suddenly, he came to life and crawled out of an imaginary thicket while looking upward at a balcony that only he could see.

"But soft!" he exclaimed. "What light through yonder window breaks?" A huge smile spread across his face as he continued, "It is the east, and Juliet is the sun!" That 100-megawatt smile stayed with him throughout his entire monologue, even as he demanded, "Arise, fair sun, and kill the envious moon . . ." while stamping the stage with his foot in its bright orange tennis shoe. "It is my lady, O, it is my love!" he concluded, with only a slight rolling of the eyes.

While the judges complimented him on his splendid performance, he shyly kicked the stage with one foot, and then the other, before half-skipping, half-running back to his seat in the audience.

"How embarrassing," he muttered, even as his buddies high-fived him all the way down the row. But that 100-megawatt smile was still with him, and that told the real story.

As I stood downstage right, holding my clipboard and watching Eduardo scurry back to his seat, I thought about what a long way we had come. Twenty-eight years earlier, my husband Bob and I had founded a nonprofit organization we called "City Hearts," dedicated to bringing the arts to underprivileged, at-risk kids. As attorneys working in the Juvenile Division of the Los Angeles County Public Defender's office, we had seen the worst of what could happen when children lived in abusive, degrading, or hopeless situations. To offset this, we wanted to give kids like Eduardo creative opportunities they wouldn't normally ever have had. We wanted to show them positive role models and offer them imaginative and productive ways to use their free time. Our goal was to show these children that there were other choices they could make—positive ones—and to help them design a vision of a future that included their creativity and held no bounds.

Beginnings

The seed of the idea that eventually resulted in "City Hearts: Kids Say Yes to the Arts" was planted when I was six years old and my parents enrolled me in private ballet lessons, which were given to me for free in exchange for publicity photos my father had taken of my teacher, a renowned Russian dancer. Lots of little girls took ballet lessons back then in the 1950s. Everybody (or so I thought) had a pair of pink tights, a black leotard, and some pink leather ballet shoes stuffed in the closet somewhere. They may not have kept up for long with their lessons, but at least these little girls had the chance to see if they liked it or not.

As for me, I happened to *love* it. I couldn't wait to pull on my tights, put my hair back in a bun, and race off to that magical place where beautiful music and graceful movements reigned. I picked up the intricate steps pretty quickly—although not fast enough for my taste. The only way to get better, I knew, was to go to class every single day. Unfortunately my parents, who were always tight on money, couldn't afford to give me extra lessons, which I really felt as such a loss. Maybe I couldn't have put it into words back then, but I was slowly forming the belief that the arts ought to be a "given" in every child's life. No one, I thought, should be deprived of dance class or art class or anything else they really wanted to study just because of a lack of money.

Partly because of this belief and partly because I was a born teacher who loved ballet, when I was eleven years old I set up my own Saturday morning ballet class for any neighborhood children who wanted to come. The lessons were held in our garage. My father would move his car, and I'd wipe up the oil from the floor and set up my record player and ballet barre. I charged my students the grand sum of 50¢ per class and the lessons were a hit. Soon, kids who had never danced before were doing *chassés*, *chaînés* turns, *changements*, and *jetés*, just like "real" dancers.

Then one day, two girls and a boy from the same family told me they wanted to come to class but their parents couldn't afford the $1.50 tuition necessary for three kids. It didn't seem right to me that they should miss out just because they couldn't pay. So I did what dance teachers and dance schools have been doing for decades: I gave them "scholarships" and let them take their lessons for free. To me it was crystal clear: the arts should be provided, *no matter what.*

I studied ballet seriously until I was about fourteen under the tutelage of Juliette Durand, a wonderful teacher and fantastic dancer in her own right. But when she moved back to New York, I had to cast about for another mentor—one that I never found. So by the time I was seventeen, I was mostly just dancing for fun, having shelved the idea of becoming a professional ballet dancer.

Once I realized I was not going to be a prima ballerina, I decided to become a doctor and entered UCLA as a premed student majoring in bacteriology. At the time, feminism was a brand new concept, and the idea that women could become doctors was not widely accepted at all. In fact, when I met the head of the Bacteriology Department, he shook my hand and said, "Nice to meet you. And I'll never see you again because you're going to flunk out of school."

As it turned out, he was very nearly correct. In short order, I flunked chemistry and was put on academic probation. As part of my probation, I had to take a battery of tests designed to help me answer the question, "What do you want to be when you grow up?" The same two answers kept popping up: doctor or lawyer. Since I obviously wasn't going to be a doctor, I opted for the latter.

It was a bit of a struggle, but I got my law degree in 1974 and passed the bar exam on the third try. By this point, I had acquired a husband, a lawyer like me who had been a year ahead of me in law school. He was already working in the Los Angeles County Public Defender's office, which sounded like an interesting place to be, somewhere I could help people. As soon as I passed the bar, I applied, but even though I scored very high on their test, the public defender's office couldn't take me on because they were in the middle of a hiring freeze, due to the state of the county budget. So I spent my first year as an attorney working in debt collection in the legal department of a major Los Angeles bank. It was absolutely the wrong job for me: I wanted to *help* others, not squeeze them for money! After a year, thankfully, the hiring freeze was lifted and I was able to become a public defender, the job I really wanted.

What If He'd Found the Piano First?

New attorneys in the Los Angeles County Public Defender's office begin by working with the juvenile clients, which was fine by me since I'd always been interested in kids. But my introduction to Central Juvenile Hall in downtown Los Angeles was something of a shock. A huge facility, it was one of the oldest and most over-crowded juvenile detention facilities in the country. As soon as I was hired, I was given a tour of Juvenile Hall with the other newly hired PDs (as we were called) and got a real sense of what it must be like to be locked up in that place. As I surrendered my driver's license and heard the metal gates clanging shut behind me, I was almost overcome by the smell—a combination of sour milk, disinfectant, and oranges. Feelings of dread, despair, and hopelessness settled over me like a dark cloud.

Our tour guide, a guard, took us through the facility, showing us the classrooms, holding cells, dining room, and dormitories. At one point, we found ourselves outside on a field where a number of very large boys were lifting weights and playing basketball. As I stood there idly watching them, I suddenly became aware of the sound of beautiful piano music carried on the air from far away. Captivated by the music and curious about its origin, I abandoned the group and followed the sound to a tiny storeroom tucked away in the corner of a nearby building. A thirteen-year-old boy in an orange jumpsuit was playing Mozart on an old piano, while a young woman, obviously his teacher, stood by, watching. I leaned against the wall and just listened to the music, which was extraordinarily peaceful, until a bell rang and the boy jumped up and went off to rejoin his unit.

The young woman looked at me, shook her head, and said, "Can you believe it? This is his *first* lesson." She then told me that all she had done was play a simple little Mozart tune on the piano and instantly the boy picked it up by ear. Then, all on his own, he started improvising, and the beautiful music I'd just heard was the result. In short, he was a prodigy.

"Unfortunately," she continued, "he committed a murder, so he's in here waiting for placement in the California Youth Authority."

I felt as if someone had punched me in the stomach: the California Youth Authority is a prison for kids. Stunned, I walked away thinking, "Damn, damn, damn! What if he had found that piano *first, before he found guns and gangs?*"

That thought was just a seed, but it began to grow as I plunged into my work with juvenile clients. I met and represented so many children who had loads of potential but *no* sense of their own creativity or why that creativity might be worth anything. The kids would tell me amazingly inventive alibi stories, and I'd think, "She should be a writer," or "He should be an actor." Some of them would draw me incredible pictures of cars or monsters, yet they knew nothing of the arts. One boy drew me such a fantastic picture of flowers that I said, full of admiration, "You could be an artist." He looked at me blankly and asked, "What's that?"

Around this time, I had opened a ballet studio at my home in Topanga Canyon and, again, was working with neighborhood children during my free time, something I still do to this day. But the difference between my students from affluent Topanga Canyon and the kids I encountered as a PD was stark. The kids in my ballet class all had parents who schlepped them to the studio, paid me, and had a real sense of responsibility and commitment to the arts. But the kids in Juvenile Hall never had these kinds of opportunities. I couldn't help wondering what would happen if they did.

Something *had* to be done.

All Things Wise and Wonderful

I met Bob Jason, the man who would eventually be my husband and partner in the dance of life, as soon as I joined the public defender's office. Bob was also a PD, but he'd been at it for nine years by that time, so he was given the task of mentoring us newbies, in addition to his regular duties. At one point, when he presented a lecture on how to write and file certain kinds of motions, I just sat there staring at him, spellbound, not hearing a word he said. I liked his hands, his face, his intelligence, and his niceness; in fact, he attracted me in every way imaginable. He was a little older than me, he was wise, and as it turned out, he had a kind and loving heart. I would eventually discover that when I stood next to him, I felt like I could breathe; I felt healthy.

All the new lawyers, including me, asked him endless questions, and ever helpful and generous, Bob was always there for everybody. He and I began to go to lunch together and discovered that we could talk to each other for hours. The turning point came when we went on a field trip with a small group of lawyers to see a probation camp and we stopped along the way for a picnic. At some point, maybe during the picnic or maybe afterward, we fell in love. Not long after, we moved in together and eventually married. (We recently celebrated thirty-six years of partnership and love.)

Bob was, and continues to be, driven by an all-consuming interest in people. Being a public defender is definitely his calling within the law, but he would be the first to tell you he has never been very interested in the *law* part of it . . . the rulings and the cases. Bob's true passion has to do with the *people* part of being a PD and the impact the system has on those people. He's totally fascinated by his clients. He'll often say, "Their lives are just so extraordinarily rich and difficult—in ways that I can hardly comprehend, because I don't have to deal with those kinds of things."

The more time Bob spent working with juveniles, the more he realized that the incarceration of children was shortsighted and an incredible waste of human potential. In our current system, *prevention* of crime or delinquency is basically ignored; it's all about *cleaning up* the mess that's already been made. And that cleanup process costs an incredible amount of money, actually much more than it would take to send that child to Harvard for the same amount of time! Bob also saw the problem of drug abuse and crime as being contagious and generational. As a PD, he had represented three generations from the same family over time: grandfather, father, and son. Wouldn't it be smarter to take some of the money spent on incarceration and invest it in at-risk kids *before* they got into trouble, so they would at least have a chance to take a better path?

There was an idea that was simmering inside of us: maybe we

could use the arts as a vehicle for prevention and intervention. As Bob put it, "The kids all have amazing potential . . . if they just get some direction in their lives. But usually they don't have good role models—parents, peers, or teachers. Without role models, they don't know what the choices are. And if they don't know what the choices are, they can't make a good choice, so they end up making the easiest choice or the worst choice."

At this point, we knew we wanted to create a program that would help underprivileged, at-risk children. But we still didn't know how.

The Birth of "City Hearts: Kids Say Yes to the Arts"

By 1984, I had been in delinquency defense for seven years; seven years of working with kids who had been given a raw deal in life and were sinking fast, with no real hope of rescue. Bob and I were married by this time and still thinking about how we could help kids through the arts, specifically dance, since I had so much experience in that area. Then one day a friend came to us with an investment opportunity. He had a building in a run-down area of downtown Los Angeles that he was turning into an artists-in-residence building. Would we consider investing in it? Intrigued, we went to take a look.

The cavernous building, situated right next to Skid Row, was built back in the early 1900s to house the Challenge Cream and Butter Company. Inside, it had corrugated roll-up doors where the dairy trucks used to pull in, and pipes running along the ceiling where hoses had dropped down to fill the trucks with milk. At one end of the building, there was an elevated area (formerly a loading dock), and as soon as Bob and I saw it we knew it would make a perfect stage! And the two giant concrete pillars that sat on either side of it could be made into a wonderful proscenium. It was, quite simply, the ideal place to set up a dance studio/rehearsal space/performance hall: a home for the arts program we'd been dreaming about. The very next day, we took out a fifteen-year lease on the building, even though we hadn't even started to create our program.

As Bob likes to put it, "We had no business plan. We had no programs to offer, no idea what we were doing or where we were going. But we put every penny we had into the space. We borrowed money from family. I even cashed in my entire pension—$30,000 back in those days—to get us going."

Much of that pension money went to pay for a 3,000-square-foot raised, padded oak dance floor. The floor was really important since we were going to offer dance classes. The original floor had a concrete base and if we had just put wood on top of it, the dancers would have been jumping on concrete, which is terrible for the joints (and really hurts!). So we had rubber pads installed every eight inches between the oak floor and the base, so that the floor never touched the concrete. We called our new place the "Downtown Dance Studio/LA Fringe Theater," and it included bathrooms, a small work area, and a separate 1,000-square-foot apartment destined for a future residential manager.

As soon as the studio was in working order, I set about finding needy children to participate in our program. Bob had seen a newspaper article about a grammar school that was opening on Skid Row, so I called the principal and said, "If you can get your kids to our studio, we'll give them free dance lessons." The principal was happy to bus over a group of sixty kids, which I then broke up into smaller groups. They became our studio's first ballet students, and I taught them myself. Our dream of helping underprivileged, at-risk kids was finally becoming a reality!

Reaching Out

Eager to help as many kids as possible, I began contacting any organization in the area that worked with impoverished children: Union Rescue Mission Girls Club, Para Los Ninos, a hospital that offered daycare to neighborhood children, and shelters for homeless people or for women with children. Each time I would tell them, "If you can get the kids over here, we have arts programs for them. For free."

Word got out and soon other groups started calling *us*, so we started adding more and more classes to the schedule. We offered any class that would get the kids to participate: dancing, guitar, even juggling and other circus arts taught by a real circus performer. Bob named our program "City Hearts: Kids Say Yes to the Arts" to honor and celebrate the fact that children *are* the city's heart.

For the first two years we financed everything ourselves, renting out our space to dance companies and offering adult classes during the day to help pay the bills. We absolutely loved it and were there every single night, rushing over after a long day's work at the public defender's office, then driving back to our Topanga Canyon home late at night. Before long, however, it became clear that we couldn't afford to keep paying all the bills out of our own pocket. It was time to create a nonprofit organization to allow for public interest and support. Bob and I found out what we needed to do to qualify as a nonprofit organization, and we assembled a board of directors, made up mostly of our friends. We learned how to write grant proposals and we plunged headlong into the world of fundraising, proudly securing our first grant: it was $2,000.

As the program grew, we soon realized there wasn't enough space in the Downtown Dance building to accommodate all the kids who wanted to participate. At the same time, after-school buses became a casualty of budget cuts, so kids who weren't within walking distance were simply out of luck. Because City Hearts was now receiving grants, we were able to hire teachers and send them out to a few schools in low-income areas. I put "dance, drama, voice teachers needed" ads in the *LA Weekly* and, later, on Craigslist. I then carefully interviewed each candidate, because we believed that the teachers were the single most important element in the entire program. I made sure that each and every one was special and had had experience working with troubled kids. All of our teachers had to be working actors, musicians, or other arts professionals. But most of all, they had to have a big heart; be a brilliant teacher able to share their passion, talent, and love of their artistic discipline; and care deeply about the lives and futures of our students.

"Sentenced to the Stage"

By 1993, Bob and I were ready to take it up a notch. Up to this point, we'd been focused on prevention and intervention, solely targeting at-risk elementary school kids. We were now convinced that the arts were so transformative they could work with kids who had *already* made bad choices—the kind of kids that Bob and I worked with on a daily basis.

To this end, we came up with a program for older kids who were on probation for nonviolent offenses and about to be ordered to do community service. Performing community service usually means cleaning up graffiti, picking up trash, and so on, but we had a better idea. What if the kids were "sentenced" to a City Hearts drama or art program instead? To find out, we put together a program called "Sentenced to the Stage" and presented it to the LA district attorney's office, the city attorney, the head judge of the Juvenile Court, the Sheriff's Department, LAPD, the Probation Department, and others.

"At that time," Bob recalls, "the system was so broken, and both delinquency and incarceration were up. So they said, 'Oh, what the hell. Nothing else is working; let's try it. Go ahead.' We were on!"

One of the boys "sentenced" to our program was a graffiti artist named Tommy (that's not his real name). At first, we put Tommy into an art program because we thought that was what he wanted to do. But somehow he got drawn into the theater program where he found a mentor, our resident manager and drama teacher who was an actor/director with his own theater company. Pretty soon, Tommy was reading and performing Shakespeare. No, Tommy didn't become a famous actor, but he did start going to school. And, lo and behold, there he discovered that he was almost a prodigy in math, something he never knew because in the past he had never gone to math class—or practically any other class either.

The upshot of it was that not only did Tommy finish high school, he eventually got a bachelor's degree from a prestigious California state university. Today, Tommy works in the IT department of one of the world's largest management consulting firms. And he gives back to City Hearts by serving alongside us on our board of directors.

Slippin' into Darkness

In the wake of our success with "Sentenced to the Stage," we decided to go even further—this time, we wanted to reach out to teens on their way to becoming hard-core criminals. The kids at Camp Miller, a military-style probation camp just one step away from the California Youth Authority, were rival gang members from rival races. They hung out exclusively with their own gangs and hated anyone who wasn't one of them, just like inmates in a state prison. Most of these kids had been involved in criminal activity and given probation, then screwed up again, resulting in a trip to Camp Miller where they typically spent six to nine months learning to fight brushfires.

It took months to convince the staff at Camp Miller to let us set up a drama program. But finally, we were given sixteen kids for a program that lasted over four months. At first, these kids, who were from rival gangs and races, didn't want to have anything to do with each other. The unspoken rule was simple: you do *not* associate with a rival gang member; and if you do, your own gang will straighten you out. But through the tremendous efforts of their talented City Hearts teacher, the boys were able to let go of their hatred and come together in an artistic endeavor, writing and performing a play about gangs (including songs) called *Slippin' into Darkness*.

Bob and I were in the audience when the boys performed their play for the other toughened Camp Miller inmates. At first there were hoots and giggles from the crowd. But by the end of the play, there was total silence except for sniffling sounds, because many of the boys in the audience were in tears.

Even after the play had faded into memory, the bonds between the boys who participated remained strong—even stronger than the bonds they had with their own gangs. They would hang out together, even at the risk of their lives. And when a fellow gang member said to one of them, "What are you doing with him? That's going to get you killed," the reply was always, "This is my brother. Leave me alone."

The Shakespeare Challenge

Over the years, Bob and I have found many ways to bring the arts to children, but one that we are particularly proud of is "The Shakespeare Challenge." Each year, more than 225 elementary, middle, and high school kids from underprivileged areas participate in Shakespeare workshops taught by City Hearts professional actors and instructors. There the kids learn history, vocabulary, stagecraft, creative movement, and depending on how old they are, they may even be trained in stage combat. The kids prepare Shakespearean monologues and scenes, which they perform at a beautiful outdoor theater in front of an audience of judges, community leaders, and families.

In the end, of course, our goal is not to turn our students into professional Shakespearean actors, professional musicians, circus performers, or famous playwrights. We just want them to discover their own potential, to dream, and to strive for a better future. In the process, we too have learned to see *our own* potential, to dream, and to strive to create a better future for the precious children in our program. We've had the incredible joy of seeing our vision become a reality, and over the years we have reached out to more than 35,000 at-risk and needy children.

Standing there, downstage at the Will Geer Theatricum Botanicum holding my clipboard and watching Eduardo, I had to admit that our journey hasn't always been easy. But it has always been rewarding. What we have learned and witnessed time and time again is that you *can* transform your life, no matter what your background or influences. It all begins with a vision of the future. Once you can envision a change, you're already halfway there.

OUR LETTER TO HUMANITY

Dear Partners in the Dream,

The program "City Hearts: Kids Say Yes to the Arts" grew out of a love story. We met in the Los Angeles Public Defender's office, Juvenile Division, and fell in love with each other and with the pursuit of justice in an unjust world. We understood that children trapped in a cycle of poverty and delinquency need to discover their own creativity, talent, and voice in order to change their community and our world.

We saw that the process of using our talent for the transformation and benefit of humanity is a path, one that starts with the first step. That's all it needs—the first child given a vision of her or his place in the world, the proverbial pebble in the pond. One child transformed becomes a ripple in the sea of humanity, with untold benefits spreading far and wide, and for an entire lifetime.

The talent and passion to implement change in the world resides within us all. It just takes a spark to step out onto that path. In our lives, the arts are what illuminate this magical path, and our capacity to be transformed by this light is what makes us human.

So our message to humanity is this: find your path, and put your talents to work. Take the first step and be the pebble that can help transform this amazing planet that we all share.

For us, City Hearts is about saving lives . . . helping to guide children toward their own creativity and sense of purpose and toward respect for life, for humanity, and for our wondrous earth. Our journey is about love, caring, empowering, and transforming, and to date, over 35,000 at-risk children have been given the opportunity to discover the talents and creativity that we all possess within us. These children step into the world not only with enhanced self-esteem, understanding, and discipline but also with a joy for learning and the vision to make a difference.

We thank *Talent for Humanity* for this opportunity to share our story, and to inspire you, we hope, to put your heart and your talent into the world.

With much love and appreciation,

—Sherry & Bob

Rise!

by ALIZA HAVA

It seems that our world today may be dying
of a broken heart. But if people's hearts can heal,
perhaps then true peace will be really possible.

I started writing songs about making the world a better place when
I was very young, only nine years old. The songs I wrote were about
kids living on the streets, about ending violence in families, and
about changing the world for the better. Of course, I didn't know
then that music was to become a defining part of my life or that I
was going to be a recording artist and a concert producer. I just did
it because it felt right.

Growing up in New Jersey in the 1980s, I was very much a
product of "pop culture," and I listened to Madonna, Michael
Jackson, Cyndi Lauper, and all kinds of pop music. While my
childhood interests were typical, I was actually picking up on a lot

that was going on in the adult world. My grandparents on both my mother's side and my father's side were Holocaust survivors who escaped from concentration camps while World War II was still raging. So I suppose it was inevitable that I would hear about the Holocaust during my childhood, especially because my mother is a Holocaust educator who fights against the belief that "it never happened." But still I couldn't bear listening to those stories, and I would shut my eyes and ears to them.

Home life was difficult. Everyone in my family always seemed to be fighting with one another. My father was busy running a business, and my mother seemed oblivious to my sisters, my brother, and me, so we were pretty much left to our own devices. As soon as we came home from school, we sat in front of the TV and stayed there until it was time to go to bed. I'm not saying there was no love there, just that it was hard to find.

At school I got picked on because I was overweight. I was beat up, spat on, called names, and made the target of cruel jokes—and I responded in kind. I could see that people were mean when they didn't need to be and could hurt others without the slightest regret. But most of my teachers never did anything about it, so I saw there was injustice in the world as well. I wanted to make some kind of a statement, even though I didn't know what that was at the time. I guess that's why I started writing songs about changing the world— it was my way of dealing with what I was going through. Then, as suddenly as I had started, I stopped writing songs and forgot about it completely.

Around the same time, I developed major issues with authority. It was clear to me that many of the adults around me were not paying attention, and I couldn't trust them. I didn't feel safe. Luckily I was given guidance here and there by a few wonderful people, including some lifelong friends of our family, who took me into their home for about nine months when I was ten years old. As it turned out, this was the very best thing that could have happened to me at the time. They didn't own a television, so I spent no more endless hours staring at the tube. Instead, they had plenty of books, and I became an avid reader. But even more important was the fact that they had very strong principles. I learned what it meant to have structure in the family, to experience discipline tempered with love. And that was exactly what I needed. Eventually, I moved back home, but I knew by then that I didn't have to make the same choices my family was making. I'd seen for myself that there were alternatives.

At the start of the new school year, when I was eleven years old, I joined the choir and developed a close relationship with a new music teacher who was different from any teacher I'd had before. He spoke to us as if we were his friends and taught us modern songs. He told us about Dr. Martin Luther King Jr. and the civil rights movement. I was fascinated, having never heard of "protest" or organized movements against injustice. Our music teacher created a show that highlighted various aspects of the protests in the 1960s, including stories from Dr. King's life and about his assassination, and we performed it for the entire school. It was a powerful experience, one that made a deep impact on me. Then a few weeks later, we found out that he was being fired. We weren't told why, but I had a strong sense it was because he'd gone against the status quo. I urged my fellow students to band together and stand up for him. That very day, I led a "sit-in" in the hallway outside the principal's office with about twenty kids, all of us refusing to move until the administration promised not to fire our teacher. It was my first taste of being an activist.

Music came back into my life, in a major way, a year later when I was twelve and I asked a friend to teach me to play the piano. My favorite song was "When the Children Cry," and I wanted to learn how to play it because its message of hope spoke to me so deeply. I didn't realize it at the time, but it was this song that inspired me to become a musician. I performed it in the eighth grade talent show, the first time I ever sang solo for an audience. Then, at fifteen, I bought an old guitar for $20, taught myself to play, and started writing songs again. Less than a year later, a music industry professional heard me sing. He took me aside, gave me his card, and said, "Wow, kid, you're really good . . . Call me when you're ready." That was the first time I realized I had a gift.

At home, things continued to be just as bad, and I was turning into a wild child. Nobody could restrain me: I was staying out late, cutting class, and basically doing whatever I felt like. I didn't really fit in, and I hated high school. I couldn't see any point, and all I really wanted was to drop out. After awhile, it wasn't just that I no longer wanted to be in school. I no longer wanted to be on the planet. I simply didn't feel any desire to live.

At the same time, I knew I didn't have it in me to take my own life. *And* I had the profound feeling I was meant for something greater—there was some reason I was here on earth. But what was it? There I was, almost at the end of my senior year in high school, crying out to God, "Please help me. I don't want to be here anymore. Why am I even alive?" Not that I really thought God was listening. But then I got an answer, and it came in a very unusual way.

Be Here Now

One day, after I'd cried myself to sleep the night before, my brother handed me a book he thought I would like. It was this funky, hippie-ish book about spirituality, yoga, and meditation called *Be Here Now* by the spiritual teacher and yogi, Ram Dass. The book reads as if you were flipping a pad on an artist's easel, and the pages looked like they were cut from a brown paper bag. Each one had an illustration on it—some of them were really beautiful drawings. The entire book looked like it had been written by hand.

I took the book to school with me, cut class as usual, and read the whole thing from cover to cover. Flipping through it was like having a conversation with someone who was trying to convince you that you were an eternal soul. Maybe it was because I am a very visual person, or maybe because I was in the perfect state of mind to get the message, but I had an unexpected and profound reaction.

The next day when I woke up I felt like a completely different person. It seemed that every single particle in the world was somehow *connected, conscious,* and *alive.* I felt my third eye was wide open, and I could see, feel, and hear what the people around me were feeling and thinking. I was in a heightened state of awareness and felt absolute, total compassion for everyone around me. I could sense the presence of some higher intelligence at work and experienced a deep, blissful state of joy, combined with the realization that everything was perfect and *exactly* as it was meant to be.

At one point I remember being in the kitchen watching my father prepare food. Instead of seeing him as "my father" with all the drama and projections of our relationship, I saw him as a human being struggling with his own issues and doing his best to get through life. I had a deep sense of detachment from the world, while at the same time being completely surrendered to it. I suddenly understood that this life is an illusion and even the struggles we face are meant to be, in ways we cannot fathom. I felt a complete sense of knowing that the universe is constantly evolving toward perfection, and for the first time, it was clear to me that what we human beings see in this world is just *one* dimension of reality. What I hadn't been aware of, until then, was that there is *so much more.*

I had the most beautiful feelings, too, of bliss and compassion— feelings I'd never had before—and this state of consciousness lasted for *two whole weeks.* During that time I became a completely different person, totally immersed in what I later learned is called "God consciousness." I felt the presence of God everywhere, along with powerful feelings of unconditional love, compassion, and forgiveness. It had become clear to me that I was an eternal being, and that my current life was only one of many I had experienced before—a fragment of time in a greater story that was unfolding.

The experience was so powerful and real that I felt the need to share my newfound understanding of life with those I cared about. But, to my surprise, most of them were pretty unimpressed, saying something to the effect of "you sound like a nut job." But I felt *they* were the ones who were nuts, because they believed that this life was the be-all and end-all of existence.

I guess it had to end eventually. I know exactly what wrenched me out of my state of bliss. I was trying to share this amazing feeling with some friends at a picnic. There was a person there who I knew was arrogant, but I thought somehow I could reach him. He listened for a while and then totally flattened me. He said, "You're a fool to believe in God. There is no God. It's all in your mind." I got very upset and went on the defensive: "Of course there's a God! Just look around you! Maybe if you stopped being so arrogant you would see that the world is full of beauty and you sure aren't the one responsible for that!"

As soon as those words escaped my mouth, my blissful state completely disappeared. It was as if the gates to heaven on earth had suddenly slammed shut, and—metaphorically speaking—I had been kicked out of the garden. I prayed to God to bring me back to that place and, in a way, that's the point when my journey really began— my journey back to unconditional love. When my prayers didn't work, I went back to the book, thinking it worked once, why not again? But it didn't happen.

In my quest to return to "God consciousness," I studied compara-
tive religion, but even after reading the sacred texts of Hinduism,
Christianity, Buddhism, Taoism, and more, I still hadn't found what
I was looking for. So, in my own way, I asked God to show me where
to look. After awhile, what became clear to me was that I was supposed to embrace the fact that I was Jewish, which had been so hard
because of all the pain associated with my family and the Holocaust.
I also felt that the Orthodox Judaism I had been exposed to as a
child lacked a sense of spirituality and was more about dogmatically
following religious law than experiencing an intimate personal relationship with God. My parents had also turned away from religion
when I was very young, and as a result, we were rejected by our
extended family. I didn't know I wanted to be Jewish, but I kept getting a sense that I needed to travel to Israel if I was going to continue
my spiritual journey and find the answers I was looking for.

It was about a year later when I was nineteen and I visited Israel
for the first time that everything began to make sense. I was reading
the passage in the Old Testament in which the disbelievers said to
Moses, "Where is your God? There is no God! There are no miracles!" Moses got angry and struck a rock with his staff to draw water
from it and prove the existence of God. And what was his punishment? He was not allowed to enter the Promised Land.

What did Moses do that was so wrong? He got *angry*, just as I
had done with that boy at the picnic. I had experienced heaven on
earth, but I got mad trying to prove the existence of God. I was
the one who had been arrogant. Had I been compassionate toward

him, I would have stayed in my state of bliss. But I wasn't. I judged him as he was judging me. And the beauty was lost. And so I had another conversation with God. I said, "I screwed up. I'm sorry. I know now the only reason I'm here is to serve You. So what do You want me to do? I'm Yours. Please show me." And that's when things began to shift.

Not long after that, I heard of a Hebrew phrase that captures an important concept in Jewish religion—*Tikkun Olam*. It means "repairing the world." The idea is that we are all cocreators of the world with God and it's our responsibility to restore it to its original form, which is Eden-like. When I heard this phrase for the first time, shortly after I had prayed so strongly, it made complete sense. I had always felt there should be justice and healing and that people should help each other, and now I felt I had a responsibility to do something to make a change. That's what kick-started my journey as an activist.

Action for Peace

I had already produced my first event to support a cause when I was seventeen, about a year before I experienced my spiritual awakening. My teacher had asked me if I'd help him organize something for Earth Day at our high school, and I immediately suggested we put on a concert. Without even knowing what I was getting myself into, we started putting together an Earth Day concert. The whole school came. I sang and played my guitar. My sister and I usually didn't get along, and yet we even performed a song together. It was a big success and one of the reasons I decided to stay in school. It gave me a sense of purpose when I saw that I could do something I enjoyed—and make a difference at the same time.

At that point in my life, I certainly didn't expect to become a producer of cause-related events or, for that matter, a recording artist. I had decided to go to college to become a music therapist, figuring that I might eventually find a clinical job somewhere. Then, during my first year in college, I performed in a music therapy concert with other students, and the school's vocal teacher came up to me and said, "You have a very good voice. I'd like to work with you and help you make your voice even better." I ended up taking four semesters of voice lessons and changing to a double major in music therapy and classical voice performance.

Although I was concentrating on music and performing during my college years, I didn't forget my wish to do something for the world. I joined a few activist clubs on campus, including Students for a Free Tibet. I became close friends with the president of the club and we decided to organize a benefit concert for Tibet, with student bands, at a local bar. We raised $1,000, which wasn't bad considering tickets cost $3 each. It gradually occurred to me that producing benefit concerts was a great way to spread a message and at the same time raise money for a cause. Not too long after the Tibetan concert, a young woman I'd become friends with was diagnosed with leukemia. I decided to organize a benefit concert to help her pay her medical bills. It seemed like a good way for the community to come together to do something for a wonderful person, and we were able to raise a tidy sum of money for her. Even better, I know she felt loved, which was reason enough in itself. She ended up using the money to throw herself a good-bye party shortly before she passed away.

My peace work, however, really started with 9/11. I was still in college at the time. I was sitting in music theory class when the teacher announced that two planes had crashed into the Twin Towers and the university was sending everyone home. No one knew what was happening. Instead of going home, I went to a friend's apartment and we sat in front of the TV watching the towers collapse over and over again. We were in shock. But rather than sitting around feeling powerless, we decided to call a community meeting at the local "Peace Park." We made flyers and spent several hours sticking them on car windshields all over town. At five o-clock p.m., about sixty people gathered at the park to talk about what was happening. No one had all the information, but one thing was clear. It felt better to be together in community than sitting home alone watching the replays. As a community, we offered a prayer for peace.

In November 2001, friends involved in an organization called the World Peace Prayer Society invited me to sing at a post-9/11 ceremony. It was the culmination of a World Peace Walk that started at Ground Zero and ended in Washington DC. As we marched toward the White House, I was asked to carry the World Peace Flame that had been brought around the world by an Olympic runner. Afterward, standing in front of the Lincoln Memorial on the same spot where Dr. Martin Luther King Jr. had given his "I Have a Dream" speech, I was invited to sing my song "RISE," which is really a kind of prayer:

> *We will RISE now*
> *Stand upright*
> *We will burn like candles in the night*
> *We will learn to sing, not to fight*
> *Unless it's for our freedom right*
> *We will hold each other's hands*
> *Try hard to understand*
> *Liberty is our demand*
> *We are One People, One Land.*

Prayer is a very powerful thing, but it is much more powerful when combined with music—and it certainly was that day. People often underestimate the power of prayer, but I've learned to believe in it more and more because I see the way it has worked miracles in my life and in the lives of others. Imagine if all the people in the world prayed together in their own languages—not prayers from books, but prayers from the heart. Now that *would* be powerful.

After the walk, we gathered at the Vietnam Memorial. I knelt down to light a candle and my eyes looked up and rested on the name directly in front of me: Joseph *Blessing*. There were thousands of names engraved into that memorial wall, and this didn't seem like a coincidence. In that moment, I recognized that this experience and my life, in fact, were a blessing. Seeing this name before my eyes was as if God was winking at me.

Moving to Israel

Over the next few years I found myself singing at many events, including the 2005 International Day of Peace at the United Nations. However, by then I was ready for a change in my life. I realized I needed to go back to my roots and decided to move to Israel. I became an Israeli citizen and soon got involved in organizations that were working toward peaceful coexistence between Arabs and Jews.

The following year, I was approached by an organization connected to the United Nations about producing a concert in Jerusalem for International Peace Day. I plunged into the concert planning with less than three months to go, but simultaneously the Israeli-Hezbollah war broke out. As a result, the United Nations canceled the concert, claiming it was in poor taste to have a peace concert during a war. In my opinion, that would have been the *best* time to have such a concert. To make matters worse, my recording career was having its ups and downs. I was starting to wonder whether *either* of these paths was right for me.

One afternoon in 2009, something occurred that seemed like another wink from God and an acknowledgment that I was on the right path. I was at a restaurant in Beit Jala, a village in the West

Bank, at a meeting with two colleagues, one Palestinian and one Israeli. We were discussing ideas for a new project when a Palestinian man at the table diagonally across from us interrupted.

"Are you Israeli?" he asked me in English, with a thick Arabic accent.

I wasn't sure how to respond because it can be very dangerous to do peace work in the region.

"I'm American," I replied.

"I heard you speaking about peace," he continued. "Are you peace activists?"

When I said that we were, he said, with more than a hint of cynicism, "That's good. I like peace. We need it here."

We talked to him for a few minutes, and then he invited us to visit his shop to see his olivewood carvings. On the way to his store, he turned to me and said, "So, Aliza, other than being a peace activist, what do you do?"

"I'm a singer," I replied.

"Oh, that's good. I love music. What kind of music do you sing?"

"All kinds, really, but I especially like to write songs with a message."

He looked at me intently. "You're from America, but you're Israeli, too, aren't you?"

"Yes, I am," I finally admitted, feeling like it was all right to open up a bit more.

"That's good. I have many Israeli friends. Listen, I have got something at my store that I think you will like a lot. It's brand new. I just finished it today."

By then, we had arrived at the store, which was filled from floor to ceiling with hundreds of beautiful hand-carved olivewood objects. Our new friend offered us tea and then disappeared into the back room. When he came out, he was holding a wooden spoon. "What do you think?" he asked. "It's my latest design."

I was stunned. The spoon was shaped exactly like a symbol I had designed as my logo several years earlier. It was unique. I had never seen it anywhere else.

"I don't believe it!" I exclaimed. "That's my logo! I've been signing my work with this symbol for years. It's even on the cover of the journal I write in every day!"

Everyone was speechless. Then our friend took us to the packing room at the back of the store and pointed at a cardboard box overflowing with stuffing.

"You see this box? Right before I went to the restaurant today, I was trying to fit this spoon into the box to have it shipped out to be duplicated. When the postman came, I couldn't get the box to close right, so I told him to come back tomorrow. This spoon is the prototype. It's the only one and it was just finished this morning. If it had gone out today in the mail you would never have seen it. This is destiny. This was meant for you. I am sure of it."

He handed me the spoon and asked me to keep it as a gift. It was a very powerful gesture. A week later I came back to visit him and brought my journal so he could see for himself. I asked him how he had gotten the idea for it.

"I don't know exactly," he replied. "One morning I just woke up and saw this image in my mind's eye, and I had to create it. The fact that you came here to my store on the day I finished it is a sign. I will do everything I can to help you with whatever you want to do for peace here in Palestine."

To this day, this man and I are friends and this design is his best-selling product.

A Journey of Peace

By now, it seemed pretty clear that doing peace work was my calling, or at least one of them. But there's a difference between doing something you feel *driven* to do and doing something you've been *guided* to do. Sometimes I thought I was being guided a certain way, and then the universe put a roadblock in front of me. After plenty of prayer and synchronicity, the message I got was this: create a peace concert, but do it differently.

It took several years of trial and error, but I finally understood how to go about it. The goal was to create a coalition of organizations dedicated to music as a tool for social change, with people who were interested in creating peace concerts in their communities. On September 21, 2012, the International Day of Peace, my project "Peace Day LIVE" broadcast nine concerts on six continents and united fifty peace and educational organizations live via the Internet in different time zones. People all over the world came together to create these events, and despite the challenges of producing an event of this magnitude, it was an incredible inspiration, and I learned a lot about my abilities as a producer.

My success with Peace Day LIVE led me to revisit an old dream—producing a joint Israeli-Palestinian peace concert. I knew that the focus had to be completely on point if the concert was going to be effective. I had seen many organizations and producers try to hold peace concerts in the region, but they had always hit insurmountable obstacles: bomb threats, artists pulling out because of international pressure, boycott movements, and other complications. I needed to figure out how to avoid them *all*.

From the beginning, there was one thing of which I was certain. It was crucial to leave politics out of it. What is it that the people of this region have in common? What, if anything, can everyone in the Middle East agree on? *God*. I don't mean what's written about God in books, because there are always arguments about religious interpretation, who Jesus was, what *jihad* really means, and so on. I'm talking about the spirit of love and brotherhood, the Golden Rule, the highest ideals that all these books are trying to show us. *Those* are the things we need to focus on in peace concerts. Let music become the prayer that heals all the children of Abraham, with Christians, Muslims, and Jews *together*. An interfaith-based music event that celebrates commonalities instead of differences—*that* is a way to inspire peace in the Middle East. The word "peace" itself is one of the names of God. The word is "salaam" in Arabic and "shalom" in

Hebrew. It's the same root. And what better place to hold such a concert but Jerusalem, literally "City of Peace."

It was in late November 2012 when I was approached by another organization wanting to hold an event in Jerusalem as part of an international broadcast of live events around the world on December 12. Time was short, but since I had already laid most of the groundwork, I decided to go for it. I put together a team of musicians and representatives from several organizations and produced a concert called "Harmony in the Holy Land." Broadcast live via the web, it brought together Muslims, Christians, and Jews through prayer and music in Jerusalem, and linked up with forty locations worldwide. We planned two days of events and had just three weeks to raise the money, secure artists and a venue, create and distribute advertising, build a website, make a fundraising video, and do a million other things. But everything came together, and it turned out to be an awesome experience. On the first day, prayer events were held in the Old City and at sacred sites in other parts of the world, and it was called the largest prayer event in history. The second day was a fantastic concert broadcast live from the heart of Jerusalem. Both events were packed beyond capacity and live-streamed to hundreds of thousands of people. It was a dream come true for so many of us and helped create a foundation for producing similar events in the region in the future.

So now it seems my journey has come full circle. I'm still that nine-year-old kid who wanted to change the world and wrote songs about it, but now I am able to use more sophisticated ways of getting results. This I do through my own music but also by bringing artists and organizations together to create messages of peace. And so am I an artist or a producer? When people ask me this, I tell them that both are my passion, but first and foremost I'm an artist. I think I'll always be involved in creating events aimed at inspiring peace in the world, but at the end of the day I just want to be singing. I consider that music is one of the most powerful medicines of all, as long as it comes from the heart.

As Helen Keller wrote, "The best and most beautiful things in the world cannot be seen nor even touched, but just felt in the heart." It seems that our world may be dying of a broken heart. But if people's hearts can heal, perhaps then true peace will really be possible.

MY LETTER TO HUMANITY

Dear Friend,

It is a privilege to have this opportunity to share the words of my heart with you in the context of this book. I do so with great reverence for all the creative individuals who have shared their personal journeys in these pages, and I honor their struggles and courage, as I honor yours.

There is a saying: "Yesterday is history. Tomorrow is a mystery. Today is a gift. That's why it's called 'the present.'" When we look back on our lives and take account of what has shaped us—the hurts and the joys, the blessings and perceived curses, the people and communities we have known—it gives us a chance to learn about ourselves in the present moment, while at the same time it evokes a deep sense of wonder and curiosity about human nature. How do we find the inner strength to face challenging situations and overcome them, against all the odds? How do we maintain the integrity of our spirit and find the determination to stand in the face of injustice, demanding what is right, in spite of adversity? The only answer I have found, in my experience, is because of the sincere love of other human beings and of the One who has given us life—God.

When I speak of God, I am not referring to any image of

God, even though there is a wealth of mystical art produced by visionaries who have felt the essence of the Creator and sought to capture its form. Nor do I speak of God in a purely religious sense, because the God I refer to is beyond religion and beyond all the conceptual boundaries and dimensions that we simple-minded humans have continually attempted to understand and explain for millennia.

What and who I am referring to is the Universal Being of infinite intelligence that reveals itself within all of Creation through a pure loving-kindness, without which our world and its inhabitants would all surely cease to exist. In my most excruciatingly painful traumatic experiences and in my deeply beautiful, cherished moments, I have chosen to acknowledge the Source of Life, only to find the presence of Grace guiding me gently and giving me the strength to continue when I thought I had no more faith to rely on, nor any shoulder to lean on.

When I think of all that I am, and of the talents I have been given, for which I am being recognized through the Human Spirit Award, all I can do is give my gratitude to God for creating me this way, for touching me with the breath of life, for holding my hand through the hardest moments, and for blessing me with the strength, insight, and courage to conquer my fears, face my demons, and create beauty where it is most desperately needed. It is only because of this Grace that I am able to write these words. I hope you will find my story an inspiration and that your life will be touched in the same way mine has been by the powerful essence of the Great Mystery.

With love and gratitude,

—Aliza Hava

In My Own Voice

by DEEYAH KHAN

The one connecting thread has been about personal freedom,
whether it's to sing, to love, to study, to work, and to live
according to the call of our own heart, to realize our potential
in the world, or to raise our voices without fear.

Music is my home. I can take it with me wherever I go, and it brings
with it a sense of belonging. Music is exile, too. I have never been
particularly attached to places, and I've moved around a lot. So music
has been my passport—my doorway into a life I never expected.

Growing up in Norway, things were quite tough. I wasn't a blond-
haired, blue-eyed Norwegian, and there weren't many immigrants
in the country at the time, so life was pervaded by a sense that I
wasn't one of "them." Being different wasn't a good thing. There was
always this sense of "us" and "them." When I was with my parents
or among large gatherings of other South Asian people, they would

say "we" this and "we" that. Yet I never felt part of the "we" either. The only thing that made me feel as though I was really home was music. It is something I can carry anywhere, and that's what makes it part of me. If you like, it is my one and only "we."

When I was seven years old, my dad overheard me singing to myself in the playground outside our home in Oslo. He immediately called me indoors to sing again for him. The next day, he took me by the hand and walked me around the house, collecting my Barbie dolls and toys and dropping them into a black garbage bag. I followed him outside. He told me to say "bye-bye" and unceremoniously threw them away. To replace them, he bought me a small electronic keyboard and started to give me music lessons. From then on, my life consisted of school and music . . . and nothing else.

My father was very, very strict. I had to do well at school *and* well at music. Even if my throat was sore or I was tired, I still had to study music from the time I woke up until I went to bed. I was always working. To my father, socializing was time wasted. If I avoided my daily practice, I would be punished. One day I skipped practice to play football with my brother. I was caught and offered a stupid excuse. I spent the rest of the summer making up for it and worked so hard that nodules developed on my throat. As I got older I realized that none of my friends lived under such discipline, but it didn't deter me. It was odd, I knew, but even though I disliked it, it was something I respected.

My father decided I needed a music teacher, but the teachers he approached refused point blank, adamant that they did not want a female student. They considered me a bad investment for their legacy: not only was I a girl, but also I was born and raised in the West and without a doubt would prove spoiled and undisciplined. Eventually, he persuaded one of the masters of Khyal music, Ustad Bade Fateh Ali Khan, to take me on. Ustad Fateh Ali held firm to his belief about the kind of child I needed to be, and I had to work three times as hard just to be on an equal footing with the other students. But his very act of taking me on was a tacit acknowledgment that I was his disciple. The teacher-disciple relationship is as important as the subject the student is there to learn. Lessons about life are of equal or potentially greater value. After my perseverance became clear, he told me in a tone tinged with resentment, "You are my student. You're the one." It was like winning a minor war.

We would start every weekday at five a.m., singing a single note for one hour, almost as a form of meditation. And then, until I left for school, he would tell me stories. Years later, Ustad Fateh Ali told my dad that it was through teaching me that he had learned the only thing more difficult than a student finding a good teacher was a teacher finding a good student. He said he felt bad that he had made me work so hard, but at the same time he was glad to have had me as a student.

Rooted in Rebellion

From the beginning, my dad was a rebel. He was raised by his father and stepmother in Pakistan before they moved to Norway in the 1960s. My grandfather was a religious, traditional man, uninterested in any world beyond his own. He was highly respected in the Norwegian Muslim community, but his unwavering beliefs pushed my father to be everything that his father was not. My dad developed into a bit of a radical—very liberal and very open minded. He was interested in philosophy, art, poetry, politics, and dissidence, and he was determined to raise my brother and me with the same values and openness of mind.

My mother is an Afghan Pashtun who left home at seventeen after disagreeing with her parents about the man they had chosen for her to marry. Her path in life was a rebellion that matched my father's, although it was a quieter one. She went to stay in Pakistan with her sister who was a teacher at the school my father's nieces attended. He came to the village to visit his own sister and, quite by chance, met my mother. They returned to Oslo together, and my father continued his studies at university. My mother was always unsparingly generous, an ocean of love, not just for us, but for everyone who needed it. She would often be busying herself making sandwiches for the immigrant children she taught, who otherwise might have gone hungry. Also she helped in women's shelters, taking care of women who had frequently been rejected by their families, and it was through her I first learned of women who were forced into marriages, who were beaten, and who kept their silence in the name of family "honor."

My parents led a humble life in Norway. My dad's spare time was devoted to developing a new community—a cultural exchange between the community we lived in and the communities we came from. He liked brains and he liked talent, and he exposed many Norwegians to seldom-heard Pakistani and Indian classical music. Our home was intense, eccentric, and disciplined. It was a meeting place for activists and intellectuals who, each in their own individual way, were trying to shake up inhuman systems of authority or push against prevailing power structures and oppression.

It was the early 1980s, and Pakistan was under the rule of Zia-ul-Haq. In an effort to gain electoral support, Zia was compromising the rights of women by courting conservative religious parties and campaigning to confine women to "the *chador* and *char divari*"—the veil and four walls—in order to reinstate the "sanctity of the family." Women's constitutional rights were suspended, and women were once again considered lesser human beings.

Many of the women who passed through our home were fighting for women's rights in Pakistan. They were brilliant, fearless, and compassionate, full of joy and creativity despite living under the most difficult and oppressive of circumstances. By contrast, the women in the Pakistani and Muslim communities in Norway in the 1980s seemed nothing like these exuberant, dauntless women. I remember vividly that when I was nine, my dad took me to see a Pakistani classical dancer perform. She was from the same strict traditional society as other Pakistani women, but she was strong and fearless. I was mesmerized. Watching her dance, it was as if my own future opened up, and I could see that it *was* possible to be strong and feminine, powerful and beautiful, Pakistani and a woman—all at the same time.

"Take Care of Her"

I was very young, only seven in fact, when I began performing on stage, and I drew a lot of attention. The public seemed to approve, and I became some sort of unofficial face for the positive effects of immigration in a country where immigrant press was largely negative. The more I was referred to as "our multicultural girl," the prouder I became, thinking that finally I was going to be part of the "we." I imagined that somehow I could contribute toward changing the Norwegian people's attitudes to the foreigners in their midst. I practiced harder and harder.

However, some members of the Muslim community reacted negatively to my performances. Groups of men regarded as the senior, conservative delegates of the community would come to our house. They would say, "Performing like this is not acceptable. We don't even allow boys to do this. This is a dishonorable and immoral activity even for a boy—let alone a girl. So you must put an end to it." Each time my father would reply, "Thank you for your concern, but this is my daughter, and she is my problem," and then they would be shown the door.

When these men saw that my father had no intention of listening to their demands, they began to call on my grandfather. Riled by my father's refusal to bow to their requests, they voiced their disapproval even louder and told him, "Your granddaughter is behaving in a way that is bringing us all dishonor, and you most of all. You have to do something about it. *Take care of her.*"

They took it upon themselves to report to my father and grandfather what I had been seen doing. It was as though I was being policed every time I set foot outside the house. At sixteen, I had signed a contract for my second album, and often I would be spotted in the street in the company of a white male. Word that I was roaming the streets with an unmarried white man would immediately be relayed to my father and throughout the community. It would have made no difference to them that I was being accompanied to or from a studio by a manager or producer. To them it was improper, and my association with the music industry implied that I was a prostitute. The video for a single off my second album was received with vitriol; it featured a shot of my uncovered back, and the guardians of orthodoxy set off on a mission to silence me. It very nearly succeeded.

I had been invited to perform at an antiracism concert in Oslo. Quite a few of my friends were at the event, and I was determined to put on a good show, but just a few songs into my set I could see fights breaking out at the back of the crowd. Refusing to be put off, I moved toward the edge of the stage. Suddenly something sharp and stinging, some kind of chemical, was sprayed into my face, burning my eyes. Immediately, I turned my back to the audience and, as my panic mounted, I tried to signal to the band that I couldn't see a thing. My eyes stung and I couldn't open them. Tears were pouring uncontrollably down my face. I had never felt more terrified. The pain was unbearable. I had no idea what had happened or what I could do. No one in the band had seen anything happen, and they didn't understand that something was wrong with me. So I kept on singing.

The negativity aimed at me for doing what I perceived to be something positive was getting too big for me to comprehend. I never spoke to the press about being attacked, and I went out of my way to avoid talking about it in public. I was getting more and more worried that speaking out would have terrible repercussions, because it would give both the Norwegian and Muslim communities reasons to turn against one another and use my experiences as fuel for their own fears and discrimination. But most devastating of all was the confusion. Where once I had been singled out because I had done well, now my success was shameful, a disgrace. I was thrown completely off guard. I was proud of my wonderful home and family and all of the incredible, inspiring people who surrounded me. My dad was behind me every step of the way. But all the other fathers in the community were trying to stop me. Talking about it would only have led to yet more discrimination and talk of racism, so I kept quiet. But privately, my war had begun.

As a Muslim woman, even in Norway, I was now extremely exposed. It was clear that I was in real danger. On one occasion, I was threatened with a knife and, on another, subjected to a failed abduction attempt. We had to keep changing our home phone number. My parents felt unable to protect me, and it weighed so heavily on them that even my father—my indestructible, unbreakable father— began to crack. And so, several months after the attacks, threats, and harassment had become constant, I bought a one-way ticket to

London. I had just turned seventeen. My mother wept but would not stop me. "You have to go!" she insisted. The helplessness she felt at not being able to keep me safe was simply agonizing.

One day shortly before I left, I was at the post office; behind the counter was a girl about my age wearing a headscarf. She had been watching me as I stood in the queue, and when I came to the counter, she shyly asked if I was Deeyah. I inhaled heavily and steeled myself for another lecture. She leaned in toward me and looked straight into my eyes. I could barely hear her speak.

"Thank you," she said. "I just wanted to say thank you." I was shocked and stood rooted in place, staring back at her.

"I want you to know," she said quietly, "that I know it is really difficult for you. But it's just because you're the first. You have to stamp down the snow, and then we will come after you and follow you. I'm very sorry you're the first one, because it is your head that will always be the one on the chopping block. But it is going to help us. So thank you."

I started to cry. I don't know if she heard through my tears how grateful I was for her saying that to me, because it was the solidarity, support, and understanding I had desperately needed for such a long, long time.

Another Country, Not My Own

At first, the move felt like a liberation, a fresh start, and a chance to blend in, to cast off the pressures of my life in Norway and to lose myself and my history in the chaos and busyness of London. I was all alone, without any responsibilities or worries. For ten days I stayed with a distant family friend, although for fear of abusing their hospitality I spent every day trudging the streets or sitting in a café in Oxford Street pondering my next steps. Naively, I paid a huge upfront sum for an apartment in Camberwell, which was rife with crime and where my tenancy was illegal—eviction notices were piling up almost from the day I moved in. However, I had money behind me from my earnings as a recording artist in Norway, and I quickly learned to find better places and got to know London intimately.

Slowly, I established myself on the music scene. I signed to a new label in London, which enabled me to get back to writing music. My manager, Steven Fargnoli, had previously worked with Prince and Sinéad O'Connor. But in 2001 he died of cancer, which was a painful blow, because I had come to rely on him. I was producing commercial pop music, which sold well, although I could not really find any fulfillment in it, and it was motivated as much by a desire for acceptance as the need to pay my rent. I thought that as long as I behaved like everyone else and I didn't stand out, the trouble would not reappear.

But I became increasingly well known, and after I filmed a music video in which I danced with a black man, awful things began once again. Despite the fact that the video reached number one on the leading UK music video program, it was pulled from a British Asian music TV channel when staff began to receive threats for letting it air. A frightening torrent of threats quickly followed: I got countless anonymous phone calls and aggressive emails, and men jostled me in the street, hissing, "Watch your back." It all culminated in haunting, taunting threats that described in graphic detail how I was to be killed. I couldn't believe it, but everything that had happened in Norway was starting to happen again in the UK. My mother, on a visit to London, was heartbroken to see me flinch when some South Asian men entered our café because I was constantly anticipating harassment. I felt like a caged animal in the circus. My life was collapsing around me; it was both horrifying and infuriating at the same time.

I was afraid but, even more than that, I was angry. I had lost ownership of myself—yet again—and my existence was being defined by someone else's rules. Each time I was threatened, I felt as though I couldn't breathe. Each time, I tensed up as a little bit of life was sucked out of me, as if they were trying to take away my voice. Which—effectively—is exactly what they were trying to do.

And they did. Because I left again. I was simply unwilling to participate in the same old cycle. I was convinced that the only thing left for me to do was to distance myself from what my life had turned into. Already I was separated from my family, my friends, and my community. I had left my old life completely behind. The time had come for me to decide on what terms my new life was going to unfold.

Letters of Love

So I kept running. Back in 1999, Steven had introduced me to some American music business friends in Atlanta, Georgia. And that is where I fled when I could not deal with the pressure a single moment longer. It was the only place where I knew people and I could afford to start a new life, far enough away from everything else I was familiar with. In Atlanta, mentally and emotionally exhausted, I took two years to recover. These were years spent blankly pointing my eyes at the TV, welded to a shabby sofa, or lifelessly watching through the window as the wind lifted the leaves off the trees. It seemed such a strange place—an urban sprawl in the middle of nowhere, where everything was enormous and roads ran for miles and miles until suddenly a shopping mall or a gas station crawled into view. Even finding work didn't help much: I felt disoriented and isolated, going through life mechanically.

Not to make music, not even at home on my own, was a different and deeper kind of sadness. I had been creating music since I was seven. So when it looked as though music was the very source of my pain, I assumed that stopping it would ease the suffering. But like an illness with a hidden cause, it wasn't music at all that was evoking such anguish. I felt dead, and I gave in to living in a paralyzing, numbing fog. And in that fog, my life took a new direction.

Ever since I first started performing, I used to get lots of fan mail and emails. I always wrote back and often would end up corresponding with people for a long time. The anonymity of email made it easy for people to talk to me about their problems. Perhaps because

I was a bit of an outcast myself, they reckoned I wasn't so likely to judge them, which made me an obvious ear for their problems. Fans, mostly young South Asians who were having personal difficulties within their families and wider community, reached out to me for support. And these were voices not raised in anger and rage and seeking my silence, but softer voices that sought my help. That was what shook me out of my torpor.

In Atlanta I kept on corresponding with them, and then I began working with charities and NGOs that help marginalized kids and women who suffered abuse. I felt passionately about this work, and it seemed that there was so much that needed to be done to help these kids. Many of the letters I was receiving revealed serious issues that were impossible to ignore. A lot of them had similar problems: some were gay; some were being shunned just for being themselves; many of them weren't allowed to go to school. Some of these young people's fears were serious enough to send me on a frantic search for hostels or shelters for them. Often I was the first person they would contact when they were scared for their lives. I couldn't sleep because I felt so helpless, constantly wondering if I could do more.

Then there were the messages from young men facing violence, even death because of their sexuality, or young women forced into marriage, who had been raped, beaten, and abused. Through all these people's experiences ran the common calls to family honor, community values, and tradition as excuses for violence and oppression—and as reasons to remain silent. And I had had quite enough of silence and compromise. After two years, I had become increasingly angry that not enough was being done either within or outside the community to help all these young people. How could I tell young people in need of refuge or support that they should just go and deal with this on their own? No matter how unqualified I thought I was, I knew clearly that I had to do more. Being angry wasn't enough.

Taking a Stand

This was how I discovered a new sense of purpose, leaving the anger and self-doubt behind and reemerging as not just an artist but an activist. "Sisterhood" was my first very own independent initiative, a website where young Muslim girls could submit art. I knew the incredible impact that art and the freedom to be creative had made on my own life, and I wanted to establish a safe place where people with a cultural bond could relate and work through some of the challenges they faced. Shortly after it was launched, Sisterhoodnetwork.org caught the attention of the Muslim press in the UK, which issued a statement condemning the site, saying that artistic and creative expression was not an acceptable pastime for girls and women. I was enraged, but also I felt proud of what I had done. In what world does anyone have the right to stop someone else from having feelings, from having aspirations, and from sharing their thoughts?

After that, I launched "I Have a Voice," a grassroots foundation committed to raising awareness about the struggle for human rights, with a focus on violence against women. From there, it just grew.

Since then I have set up the "AVA Foundation," under which arts education, mentorship, and outlets for self-expression for marginalized children and young people are gathered, including the Honour Based Violence Awareness (HBVA) Network. In the case of the HBVA, I decided that what was needed was a comprehensive resource for information and training, and so, together with experts in the field, we created a digital resource center that provides education and training for the very individuals who are in a position to help young people at risk—for example, police, health-care workers, schoolteachers, and the like.

Then, my own experience of the attempts to suppress my music led me to take an active role in support of "Freemuse," the international organization that takes a stand against the alarmingly widespread censorship of music. This is how I came to produce a CD *Listen to the Banned*, a collection of music by banned, censored, persecuted, and even tortured artists, with the aim of highlighting the right of each and every individual to creative self-expression.

A Different Kind of Love Story

Having an outlet for women who were victims of violence, so often inflicted by members of their own family and community in the name of honor, made me toy with the idea of making a documentary about honor-based violence. I had never done anything remotely like making a documentary and had no idea how to go about it. But I contacted some people I knew in production and said, rather boldly, "I'm going to make a film." They laughed but offered to help where they could. I had no script, but I knew what I wanted to say and was determined to find the people, or the circumstances, to make the story real. I initially envisioned an educational movie that would be shown to women's groups and, at the very most, might be entered in a few film festivals. I never dreamed where it would actually take me.

Then I found Banaz. Banaz Mahmod was a nineteen-year-old woman in the UK, forced into an arranged marriage by her family. She fled the marriage and fell in love with another man, and for that her father, uncle, and a group of family friends, the people who should have loved and supported her, instead plotted and carried out her brutal murder.

In the course of my research, I met Caroline Goode, New Scotland Yard's detective chief inspector in charge of Banaz's case. I met her one afternoon to see whether she would consider being interviewed for the film. I was struck by her professional, almost stiff, demeanor. She is a ruthless detective; one does not attain her level of success by being soft and gentle. But as she spoke, her eyes gave her away. I saw that there was much more to her than just an investigator at work. She had lived and breathed Banaz's case. At the end of our meeting, she momentarily dropped her guard. "I love these women," she said. I had uncovered what would make the film more than a horror story. I had found a person who cared as much about these girls as I did.

Caroline Goode didn't meet Banaz until she dug up a suitcase in a south London backyard and opened it to reveal her body crumpled up inside. And yet she loved and cared and wanted justice for this woman, and others like her, whom she had never met. This was how the film became an unconventional love story, built on Caroline's human compassion for another woman, a compassion like my mother's, a compassion that transcended boundaries. It was as if Banaz had, I felt, been adopted and finally received some of the love and care her own family had denied her.

Banaz's story wasn't any more brutal than other stories I was aware of. But I knew I wanted to tell a story so people would see it, be blindsided by the horror of it, and then also feel compelled to do something about it. I'm not interested in victims. I never have been. Banaz is a victim only in that she is dead. She didn't live like a victim. She was making her own life, *bravely, honestly*. She inspired me the same way as when I was a little girl surrounded by the victors of adversity in my own home.

Making *Banaz: A Love Story* was life draining. It took me nearly four years. I started and stopped a lot because I didn't have enough money and would have to pause for a while and make enough to carry on. And I didn't realize that being so close to something that is so truly horrifying, for such a long time, would have such an effect on me. I became so consumed with the subject that while I was making the film, I also decided to set up "Memini," an online memorial for victims of honor killings. *Memini* means "remembrance." Many of the stories I came across were hidden deep within families. So many people knew exactly what had happened to Banaz, and they would speak to me, often sobbing over the phone, but they drew the line at coming forward and going public for fear of what the community would do to them. This made my work and the job of the investigators hugely difficult.

Girls were being killed with the intention that their deaths might also erase them from ever having existed. Many of them weren't given tombstones. I felt a nagging responsibility to set up a permanent memorial to remember them and how they had lived. All day I would film, and at night I would sit up for hours posting to the website the stories of murdered young women. It was a gut-wrenching experience.

The crime committed by each of these strong, amazing people was only to have been born a woman, and in a community that demands you live a certain way. You aren't able to choose your life, or imagine your own life, because it has been set out for you with carefully prescribed rules. These conventions don't allow women to become full human beings, simply because they are female. As a woman, the script of your life is already written, and if you misbehave then you are punished. Men will come into your home and tell you what you can and can't do. They will go to your grandfathers and fathers and uncles. And they will persist until you agree, and you are married off, or threatened or beaten into submission. If all else fails, they will kill you. Death is the final punishment, and it has been used, and it is still being used even today. I see myself in these women, and I realize how lucky I am to have a voice and to have some ability to stand in solidarity with them, by remembering those who have been murdered or by helping save others from the same terrible fate.

While I was making *Banaz: A Love Story*, I would sleep for days on end and wake up exhausted. I even started getting grey hair. In the end, I discovered that there was only *one thing* that was going to make it possible for me to finish this film, and that was to start creating, composing, and producing music once again. You see, all along—and this was the greatest irony of all—being a performer and a singer had never been my choice; it was my father's, something I did to fulfill his expectations. I went through all those hardships for a dream that wasn't even mine. However, the love that did become mine was the love of creating, composing, and producing music, which remains the only thing that replenishes and revitalizes me. So that is what I did. And now I have come full circle, rediscovering that music is for my own survival—music is what feeds me.

Epilogue

In spite of everything, I feel like I won the lottery by being born to parents like mine and into a country like Norway. But what good is my life if I don't contribute? If opportunities and possibilities are only limited to me, they are simply good luck. They have to be for everyone. Through all these events and experiences, the one connecting thread has been about personal freedom, whether it's to sing, to love, to study, to work, and to live according to the call of our own heart, to realize our potential in the world, or to raise our voices without fear. This is my story, my vocation, and my art, whatever it may require—music, activism, or documentary filmmaking, and then whatever will follow. In one way or another, now and for the rest of my life, I will keep doing whatever sheds light on these issues. For as long as I can draw breath, my voice will speak out for human rights and nonviolence. That's the only way to live life, I believe. Otherwise, we starve and we die.

MY LETTER TO HUMANITY

My letter to humanity must go to girls and women every-where, particularly to those who face violence and oppression from their very own families. I believe that every human life is sacred. Each and every one of us, simply by virtue of being born, is given a life to live out. And then we die. Yet dying, in and of itself, is not the tragedy. The tragedy is when a person's essence is not able to speak, and contribute, to this world while she is alive.

I write this letter to Banaz and those like her. I can only hope, dearest Banaz, that I have done some justice for your soul and that your story will help many, many others. My heart aches when so many of our young people are actually *forbidden*, by the very individuals who ought to be nurturing them, from forging their own destinies. Instead, they are punished, brutalized, even murdered. They are faced with a tragic, heartbreaking choice, between a life that is bleak, heartless, and constrained . . . and death.

When we fail to include, genuinely, half of the human species, it's inevitable that vital information and creativity are stolen and lost to a world that desperately needs them. Our inability to include one half of humanity robs us of strength and genius, and the world is falling apart because those pieces that are missing, those solutions that elude us, are actually held within that other half of the human family. Considering the enormous challenges facing the world today, it does not seem wise to waste a single human being, and yet we do.

When half of us are prevented from achieving our potential, then all of us, the whole of humanity, lose an incalculable treasure. When daughters are forced to restrict their boundless potential into narrow roles, humanity is deprived of its best hope for the future. And so the world is a poorer place for losing the unique talent and presence of Banaz and the millions of women like her. It is a tragedy for all of us who never met her and for a world that has lost a precious and irreplaceable individual who was just beginning to find her own voice and reclaim possession of her heart.

To you Banaz, I make a vow: I will work until my last breath to contribute in some small way toward the emancipation of girls and women and toward a world that is equitable, where freedom, dignity, and rights are respected, and where every individual can feel part of a common humanity without letting the barriers of faith, gender, or ethnicity divide us. I vow to contribute toward a future of equality, rights, and progress, a future we can all share, in which collaboration is prized over competition, inclusiveness prevails in society rather than hierarchical power structures, and dignity and compassion take the place of domination and humiliation.

So I am committed to showing up to life, living it as fully, truthfully, and lovingly as I can. All I can do is work hard and dedicate myself to taking action every single day, in the name of Banaz, and in the name of the millions of our face-less, nameless girls and women. I have not done anything to deserve to be here, so what am I going to do with the good fortune, joy, and blessing of this life that I have been granted? I am determined to do whatever I can to be of some use in the short time that I am here, to honor the responsibility I have—not just to myself, but to others as well, and especially in solidarity with the voiceless and the marginalized.

And yet my heart is filled with boundless hope when I see the courage, the creativity, and the brilliance of young people from every corner of the earth, pointing us toward a better world for our daughters and granddaughters who I dearly hope will be able to realize their full potential without fear. To realize my own potential, I had to extricate myself from a bog of pain, fear, and insecurity, and I hit a point in my life where I could no longer continue. But the pain turned out to be the birth pangs of an inner rebirth, a sense of clarity where I found my heart again and my mission in life. From that date, my art and my creativity have become the vehicle for my pas-sion, with love, freedom, and self-expression at its core.

I believe that creativity is the source of beauty and truth, social responsibility, and spiritual expression. Art, the creative process, is a way of touching the infinite, of exploring and transforming what it is to be human. For me, it is an exploration of humanity's vast untapped potential. That is why I believe that together we can reimagine and create a future nurtured by love, freedom, and equality.

—Deeyah

Connecting the Dots

by YARROW KRANER

Every human being has the right to find his or her unique gift
and the responsibility to share it with the world.

There are extraordinary people everywhere. I've spent my life finding
and connecting them. But before I could begin to do that, I had to
find myself.

For two long years, starting when I was twelve years old, I was
the only white kid living on Rocky Boy Indian Reservation in
northeastern Montana. Just as I was about to start seventh grade,
my mom and I arrived at the "Res" (as everybody called it) in a
beat-up old U-Haul truck stuffed with everything we owned. And
what we owned wasn't much: a pile of secondhand clothes, some
used toys, and a few pieces of worn-out furniture. After living in a
long series of run-down, dilapidated houses and apartments while
my mom worked her way through school, we'd finally made it to

the big time: Mom had borrowed a car and clothes from a friend for the interview . . . and she had gotten her first real teaching job, as an art teacher on the Res. When she got the news that she was hired, we were high-fiving.

Our new place was no different from a lot of the others we'd lived in: another run-down apartment on the brink of being torn down. The school I'd be going to was across the street and down a hill, and I had to traverse down a long, rickety, dangerous-looking wooden staircase to get there. The school playground started right at the end of the stairs, and I was glad to see that it was so close.

In spite of our circumstances, I was a pretty happy, friendly, fun-loving kid at that time and was looking forward to making some new friends. So when I saw two kids playing basketball on the school playground, I couldn't wait to pull the last box off the U-Haul and run down there to join the fun. As soon as I was done unpacking the truck, I hurried down those rickety stairs and shouted, "Hey, guys!"

The ball stopped bouncing and both heads turned toward me simultaneously, while two pairs of unfriendly, suspicious eyes sized me up.

I smiled and ran up to them, eager to make new friends. As I got close, a fist suddenly shot out of nowhere and BAM! my nose exploded! Before I could even take in what had happened, there was blood everywhere and tears were streaming down my face. What in the world did I do wrong? Was it something I said? Ha! Welcome to the Res, kid.

For the next two years, as the only white kid in a total population of about two thousand Native Americans, I would bear the brunt of a century of anger and resentment against white people. And there was plenty of it. The residents of Rocky Boy thought, no, they *knew* they'd been given a raw deal.

In 1902, Chief Rocky Boy petitioned President Theodore Roosevelt for a "closed reservation" for the Chippewa Cree, where the land would be preserved for them alone. Ever since, Rocky Boy has been the designated home of the Chippewa Cree Indian tribe, people who'd once lived all over Montana before being confined to less than 175 square miles of barren land—the smallest Indian reservation out of seven in the state. When I lived there, it was a pretty desolate place: unemployment was high, half the population lived in poverty, and government resources were scarce. To say that the residents of Rocky Boy were angry at whites was an understatement.

So that was the mind-set on the Res when I bounded onto the playground with my blond hair and blue eyes like some friendly puppy. Nobody in that community was ever going to take my side or try to protect me. And that meant my years there would be tough. But they would also teach me some valuable lessons.

A Long and Winding Road

The road that led Mom and me to the Res began years earlier, even before I was born. My parents were both artists, two crazy kids who met at art school in Colorado in the late 60s during the height of the hippie era. They fell in love, I guess, and Mom soon, accidentally, got pregnant. My father loved to work on huge canvases; he'd been known to knock out entire apartment walls just to get his paintings out of the place to go sell them in Chicago. When I was two years old, we lived in a violent Denver ghetto that was so dangerous my mom was afraid to go out even in broad daylight. When her parents insisted on visiting, my mom quickly rented another apartment in a different part of town for a week so we could pretend we lived there. After her parents left, my mom realized she had finally reached her limit. An hour after they were gone, she told my father she was going to the store, and with only a quarter in her pocket and me on her hip, she walked out of that apartment and out of his life forever.

Mom used that quarter to call a friend, who picked us up on a street corner and took us to her home some fifty miles away. For the next four months, we lived with this good-hearted woman while Mom worked at a Dairy Queen and scraped together $200, just enough to buy an old car. Then we were off to Minneapolis, where Mom enrolled in college. She knew it was going to be hard going, but it was time for her to make something of her life. And she had to do it on her own. Over the next several years, Mom worked three or four different jobs—maid, nanny, washing toilets, things like that— while she went to class, studied, and took care of me. And eventually she earned the first college degree in her family. Next came grad school in Bozeman, Montana, famous for its arts programs.

Obviously, money was always a problem. We lived in the worst places imaginable: decrepit apartments, tiny run-down houses in ghettos, and even places that had been condemned and were about to be bulldozed. A few generous souls took pity on us and let us stay for free in places they weren't using—summerhouses or cabins. We actually spent an entire Montana winter in a cabin in the mountains with no electricity or running water, with a wood stove as our only source of heat and plastic sheeting in place of windows. The cabin was halfway up a big hill, and we had to trudge through huge snow-drifts just to cart water into the place.

In spite of these hardships, I was content, because it all usu-ally felt like an adventure. Mom was great and I loved her a lot. I was outgoing, with a diverse group of friends, and was constantly bringing home the kids nobody else wanted to be friends with. I also liked organizing neighborhood games and making sure every-body was included. I wanted everybody to be happy and part of the group, and I tried to make sure that nobody was ever left sit-ting on the sidelines.

So things were going along pretty well for me until about the age of seven when I suddenly began to feel a real need for a male pres-ence in my life. I felt the need to be around a man, someone I could model myself on, at least once in a while. It got to the point where I started hanging out in the fishing aisle at the local grocery store while Mom was shopping, just waiting for some guy, any guy, to come in looking for fishing gear. When one did, I'd rush up to him and say, "Hey, you going fishing? You want some company? I'll go with you!" Then Mom would hurry over, all embarrassed and apolo-gizing, and drag me away. I actually did get to go on one fishing trip that way. These forays into the fishing aisle were probably what prompted Mom to enroll me in the Big Brothers program.

During those years I spent a lot of time on my own and it would have been easy for me to start heading down the wrong path and getting into a lot of trouble. But then I was "matched" with Howard, a young man who really knew how to be a big brother. Howard was the guy who taught me how to throw a football, shoot pool, watch sports, and do the kinds of things a boy wants to do with a dude. But what he was really good at was making me feel special. We got together for about an hour every week, which doesn't sound like much, but that time was transformational for me, and the positive impact he made on my life continues to this day. Howard taught me how to be kind, generous, funny, available, and interested in helping others. I'm still in contact with Howard and I hope he knows how grateful I am for everything he's done for me.

Around this time, the artistic side of my personality started to emerge. I liked to draw pictures, write poetry, and make sculptures out of junk I pulled from the trash. Somebody loaned me a cello and I started taking free lessons at school. Then, for my eighth birthday, Mom gave me my first camera, and I began to observe the world in a new way: documenting the shortcuts I took on the way to school and taking pictures of the crossing guard, the artists doing pottery at my mom's art school, and other people I saw here and there. My perspective shifted forever. It occurred to me that I could look at the world in the "normal" way—what my eye showed me—but with a camera, I could look at it in a completely different way and show others things that they didn't see for themselves. I could zoom in on the petal of a flower and see it in detail, or catch an expression on a person's face and get a pretty good idea of what he was thinking. It was the beginning of an ability to see nuance in the world around me.

But my artistic world came to a screeching halt once we moved to the Res. Suddenly, life was all about survival, and artistic self-expression was completely out: it made me too vulnerable. The kids there had inherited their parents' fury and were just looking for a target. They called me "Little Custard," a reference to Custer's Last Stand, and a pretty ominous nickname for the only white kid on an Indian reservation.

During the first eighteen months I lived on the Res, I got beat up every other day. When school ended at three p.m., I'd wait around in the classroom until all the other kids had gone. Then I'd look out the window, checking the playground and the stairs that led up to my street to see if anybody was waiting for me. When it seemed like the coast was clear, I'd make a run for it and sometimes make it all the way up the stairs without any trouble. But about half the time, a swarm of five or six guys would suddenly materialize and jump me. It got to be a game for them: they just loved chasing me home. And once they got ahold of me, it was a real free-for-all; they'd get in as many punches and kicks as they could while I curled up in a ball and prayed for it to end. I learned pretty quickly that the sooner I cried, the sooner they'd leave me alone, so sometimes I started crying before anybody even landed the first punch. Then, once they left and were a safe distance away, I'd jump up and scream, "FUCK YOU!" after them before racing up the stairs.

The teachers at school either didn't know what was going on or just turned their heads. The Res was a dead end for most and, at best, they were apathetic. I had one social studies teacher who kept a bottle of booze in his desk drawer, added it to his coffee, and sipped away all day long. He barely did any teaching, just handed out worksheets we were supposed to fill out for the entire hour. There might have been a few teachers at that school who really liked teaching, but they had a terrible time controlling the rowdy boys. And without control, it was pretty hard to get anything done.

Realizing I wasn't going to get any help from the teachers, I decided to keep my problems to myself. I didn't tell my mom, either, because it would only upset her, and what was she going to do about it, anyway? We had nowhere to go and she really *had* to make this job work. As the only white woman on the Res, she sure wasn't going to find anybody who was sympathetic or interested in helping us out. Although she didn't mention it, I knew that she, too, had to face plenty of anger and resentment on a daily basis. I'd noticed that she slept with a hatchet by her bed (the only weapon we owned). And that spoke volumes about how unsafe she felt.

Turning the Corner

A year later, I'd had enough of feeling like a scared, hunted animal, and decided to bulk up by lifting weights. Then one day, that same pack of kids was chasing me across the playground and, as usual, I was running for my life and had bounded halfway up the stairs when something just clicked in my brain. I asked myself, "What the hell am I running from?"

I spun around to face the main bully who was chasing me and kicked him as hard as I could, catching him right under the chin (a few steps down from me). WHAM! My foot lifted him into the air and he came crashing down on the stairs flat on his back. The other guys were so stunned their mouths dropped open and they stood there frozen as I jumped on top of the big guy and went crazy on him. I jumped up, and as I ran after the next two, they took off.

That was the last time they chased me. And I learned something: the more you run away from your problems, the worse they get. But once you face them head on, they have a way of disappearing. It's a lesson I've never forgotten.

Once I learned to stand up for myself, it was time to take things to the next level: I was going to make those kids on the Res *accept* me. Rocky Boy was known for its really good basketball team, so I decided to join. Unfortunately, I was the worst basketball player ever: I'd throw the ball and miss and miss and miss again. Before long, no one *ever* expected me to make a basket and I had become entertainment for them. They laughed like crazy every time I missed, which some people might have found embarrassing, but I really didn't mind. It helped me fit in a little bit, so I didn't care if I had to make an ass out of myself. And then one day in the middle of an important game, I threw the ball, watched it roll around the rim a couple of times, and—unbelievably—it went in! The audience erupted; people all over the auditorium were on their feet, screaming, *"Yeah! All right! Woo hoo."* Little Custard finally made a big splash!

We stayed on the Res another six months until I finished eighth grade, then my mom packed us up and we spent my first two years of high school in Helena. I kept growing, lifting, putting on muscle, and soon joined the football and wrestling teams, while telling my mom I was going to cross-country running practice. Then she was offered a teaching job in Bozeman, back where we had been four years earlier.

Finding My Way

Back in Bozeman, when I showed up for the first day of football practice, nobody could believe I was the Yarrow that had left four years earlier. Because I wasn't. I had grown both in physical stature and also in confidence. I had started to become a man. And then one day, at a basketball tournament, I happened to run into a couple of the kids from Rocky Boy who used to beat me up. The hair on my back started to bristle. It surprised me how small and scrawny they looked: none of them had grown much since I'd last seen them, and for a second or two I really loved the idea of retribution.

But as soon as I had that thought, another one followed it, and it was a true revelation: I understood where their hatred had come from, and I wasn't going to buy into or contribute to the problem. I had already learned that treating others badly because of their heritage or their skin color was dead wrong. And now I realized that returning those bad feelings was just as wrong.

It sounds strange, but I suddenly felt lucky. "How many white kids get to feel racism from the reverse perspective?" I asked myself. I began to realize that those terrible experiences at Rocky Boy were actually a blessing for me, because for the rest of my life I would never think about treating others badly based on race or some other way of "grouping" people. I understood that what we really need to do is *connect* with each other. It was such a powerful, transformative moment for me that I felt myself propelled forward to one of the guys, reaching out to shake his hand.

"Hey buddy," I said, in all sincerity, "I'd like to thank you."

He eyed me warily, like he didn't quite believe what I was doing. "For what?" he asked suspiciously.

I looked him straight in the eye, smiled, and said truthfully, "For teaching me a lot."

Then I walked away.

Circling Back

After graduating from high school, I went to college on a football and wrestling scholarship, still warily avoiding the world of creativity. But my heart wasn't in it. I needed a real direction, something meaningful to do with my life. But I didn't know what that was. Then one day while taking a shortcut across the Montana State University campus, I happened to wander through the Film Building. I took one look at a display of old film cameras sitting on a rack and was knocked sideways by an absolutely clear, *aha!* moment. "Oh, so *this* is what I'm supposed to be doing!" I realized. I'd been running away from the arts and creativity for six years, and I'd proved to myself a hundred times over that I could be a jock and a "manly" man. And now, at last, I could get back to what I really *should* be doing—working in the arts. That artistic kid who used to write poetry, play the cello, and look at the world through a camera lens was back.

In film school, I felt I'd finally found my calling. Using film to tell stories seemed completely natural to me and I seemed to have a talent for it. Even before I graduated, I started my own production company and began making commercials for local businesses using school cameras. I wasn't making any profit; in fact, I was putting some of my own money into those projects. But I was in "the business," doing good work and creating a sample reel that would get me other work. When the dean stepped in and put a stop to my using school equipment, I just rented a camera and had it shipped up from Los Angeles. I'd book five or six clients back-to-back, shoot the footage, ship the camera back, then go to LA to do the post-production. It was pretty hectic, but it was a start.

After a few years, I made the inevitable move to LA, supposedly the creative center of the universe, with a goal of directing commercials, music videos, TV, and films. And, like a lot of other people, I learned pretty quickly that it's hard to break in when you're just another guy with a film degree. (I can't remember how many times I heard, "You're *who*? . . . from *Montana*?") So I started work in the film industry by doing some pretty menial production jobs. But within a few years, thanks to working really hard, I caught the attention of a few influential people, and a few doors were opened for me. I found myself directing music videos, as well as some of my own projects. It was a dream come true . . . or was it?

Superdudes

When I moved to LA, I told myself I was moving to the epicenter of creative genius. I'd been living in LA for three years when I found myself standing alone on the terrace of a big house in the Hollywood Hills, looking out over the city lights. I was at a party, martini in hand, looking around and feeling dissatisfied. I stepped outside onto the deck. Seeing all those lights twinkling below and thinking about the millions of people that were out there, I remembered why I'd come to LA, thinking it was the destination for incredible people. But I hadn't met nearly as many as I'd thought I would.

I was so lost in my own thoughts that I actually wondered aloud, "Where are they?" Suddenly a stranger, who seemed to appear out of nowhere, replied, "Who?"

"Oh, I'm sorry . . ." I said, "I didn't realize I said that out loud."

We started talking. And, as it turned out, he was a Czech composer who taught deaf kids how to play musical instruments. The very next night I met a scientist who was working to repair the ozone layer. Stunned, I looked at him and said . . . "You're literally saving the world . . . is it working?" Soon I found myself meeting one amazing, creative person after another—and not at Hollywood parties! They were people I probably would have overlooked before—like a neighbor, or a checkout clerk, or the guy who delivers the mail and donates at his neighborhood community nonprofit.

Not long after that party in the Hollywood Hills, I was lying in bed half asleep when I had a very powerful vision: There were many, many twinkling points of light, like stars, just hanging in the sky that were irresistibly drawn together and suddenly started connecting like a succession of little magnets. It occurred to me that each star represented someone I had just met and brrrrrrrrrrrup! Now they were all connecting to each other, until they created a white light that exploded. I sat bolt upright in bed and thought, "Amazing people are everywhere but they don't know that other amazing people even exist! Everybody is a real-life hero in some way and everybody can inspire someone else! I've got to find a way to create a network for these real-life heroes!" It felt like I'd finally discovered the mission that had been absent from my life for so long.

Over the next several weeks I met more brilliant minds, lots of them. And later that summer in 1999, "Superdudes" was born in my garage, with a group of good friends. Our task at Superdudes was to find people who were doing inspiring and incredible things and bring them together, so they could provide a support system for each other and inspire young people coming up. We began by visiting children's hospitals, charities, and school districts, and asking kids, "What makes you Super?"

Our message was: "Superheroes aren't simply the characters we see on the big screen. They're the people we encounter every day that are making the world a better place. Extraordinary people are everywhere. To find one . . . look within."

When we encouraged people to look inside themselves, they were able to find and express qualities that enriched their lives and their communities. Every kid, no matter what their situation in life, would light up as they answered that question "What makes you Super?" By being asked to define what it was that made them super, they realized what they aspired to be, deep within—their very "best self." And they found the whole process of discovering their super-self, and then bringing that super-self to life, was immensely empowering and enlightening. Because the moment you define your "best self," the closer you are to becoming it.

Letters poured in from teachers, parents, and child psychologists. I remember one kid named Max. His mother sent us a letter telling us that once Max was "Supernated," he felt as if he could fly . . . even though he was autistic and in a wheelchair.

As we searched the world for amazing people, the community grew. These "superheroes" included educators, scientists, writers, and composers that no one would ever know about. But they were also people like the guy who bags your groceries and donates his spare time to the local soup kitchen. We wanted to spotlight these people and help everyday people realize that they were also superheroes.

They just needed to find the superhero inside them, and we could help them do that. Then they could use their "superness" to change the world just by doing little things. We worked feverishly toward these goals for four and a half years and grew Superdudes from a "garage business" to one of the earliest social network communities, made up of *almost two million* people.

We worked with celebrities, national charities, children's hospitals, and schools, to help kids achieve their potential and improve their communities. Superdudes got a prompt on their profile page—"How do you save the world? Start with where you are. Enter your zip code." When players entered their own zip codes, twenty different things would pop up that they could do in their own neighborhoods to make the world a better place. Eventually, Superdudes got thousands of people involved in walking dogs for the local humane society, spending time with the elderly, restocking books at the local library, doing park reclamation cleanups, and so on.

I remember feeling incredibly blessed, like I had found my purpose here on earth. And it helped me discover my real passion in life: connecting people, launching ideas, opening the doors of opportunity for those who want to make the world a better place, and being "a creative alchemist."

HATCHing a Better World

With Superdudes, we scraped through the dot-com bomb, 9/11, and various financial disasters, and crawled across the finish line to survival. In order to persevere, I lived homeless underneath a desk in a donated office for five months. But by 2003 and early 2004, Superdudes had become one of the fastest-growing properties for teens and tweens, and the average time spent per user on Superdudes was greater than on larger brand names on the Internet, including eBay, Yahoo, MSN, and AOL.

That's when Fox Studios made an acquisition offer. I didn't want to sell, but our investors outvoted me and Superdudes was sold. Fox then bundled us with MySpace and a casual game company and—just like that—we were done. It just sort of faded away. The studio folks saw it as some kind of media property; they didn't understand the nonprofit component and couldn't figure out what to do with it, so in the end it was shelved and it slowly died.

After Superdudes was sold, I felt like my whole purpose in life had been stripped away. I packed my bags and moved back to Montana. I felt demoralized for a couple of months until I realized that Superdudes was not the only way to accomplish this purpose; it was just one vehicle. I could still help people see their own "superness" and connect them with other amazing people. I just needed to figure out a new way to do it.

The answer came in the form of HATCH, a nonprofit organization I cofounded to connect creative minds. Our aim is "to unite, mentor, and activate innovators to HATCH a better world."

What we do is to nurture and "curate" creative thought leaders in all kinds of areas—film, music, design, photography, technology, and experience-driven arts—and match them with cross-disciplinary peers and deserving students, chosen because of their talents and their passion. At a four-day conference in Montana, we mix up these mentors and mentees. Sometimes the relationships forged there lead to collaborations and concepts that are world shifting. I've focused on HATCH for ten years now, and it has blossomed into something very powerful.

We've seen some amazing initiatives born through HATCH, such as people coming up with new solutions for disaster-relief housing, or developing tools for teaching science through creative design. The mentors and the students stay in touch and continue building a relationship that includes ongoing advice, introductions to others who can help, and so on. Since 2004, HATCH has connected over five hundred mentors with approximately five thousand students. And I've come to see and believe that creativity, innovation, and the coming together of great minds can eventually solve many of the world's problems.

Only Connect

I've been able to bring people together ever since I was a kid who organized neighborhood games and brought home the misfits. My chance reconnection with the Rocky Boy kids reminded me that connecting, and not hatred, was the way to make the world a better place. Now, connecting others has become my life's passion. People might think of me as a director because of my film work, but I'm really just a guy who connects the dots. I thrive on uncovering each person's unique story, connecting great minds, launching ideas, and creating opportunities.

And now I've spent about fifteen years connecting amazing people, first through Superdudes and then through HATCH. But I'm not done. As this book is being written and published, we're crafting our blueprint to unveil the next generation of the secret society of real life superheroes . . . like you.

Maybe someday in the future I'll wander into a sporting goods store and a little kid will run up to me and say, "Hey, are you going fishing? I like fishing! Can I go with you?" And I'll smile at him and say, "Absolutely. Let's go!"

MY LETTER TO HUMANITY

It is an honor to be included among the inspiring stories of the creative leaders that you are connecting and bringing together.

Every story of transformation is a powerful one and happens within each of us in small forms, day after day. We are in continuous transformation. However, there are certain intersections in life that catalyze transformation to such an extent that our life path, and who we are, shift dramatically.

The key is to believe. Many people think to themselves that they will believe it when they see it. I have for a very long time firmly believed that you will see it when you *believe* it. You will manifest through believing in your vision. So . . . what do you believe in? That your circumstances will improve? That there is a way out of a difficult situation? Just know that the universe wants you to succeed. But you must believe. You must envision.

Every human being and every community is born with this boundless gift.

I also believe that one of the keys to manifest a better world is creativity. Creativity is our gift; we all are in possession of this wonderful vision, but what we do with it is our own decision. Creativity is the ability to see what does not exist yet, and if we see beautiful things, then we have an obligation to share them with the world.

Creativity is a critical way of thinking differently—and overcoming challenges. Every scientific innovation, every technological breakthrough, every advance in communication, was sparked by creative thinking. The same creativity that twisted a piece of wire into a paper clip or that molded silicon into a computer chip can solve every significant problem facing the world today.

As humans we are also gifted with an incredible amount of resilience, and if we continue down our life path with belief, courage, and creativity, we will overcome any obstacle on the way to helping "hatch" a better world.

Like a seed, the human spirit needs nurturing, empowering, and celebrating to ensure the sustainability of humanity. Every human being has the right to find his or her unique gift and the responsibility to share it with the world. Every community forms a multigenerational garden where those gifts are cultivated and harvested for the common good.

The power of vision is humanity's gift to the world. Use it.

With gratitude,

—Yarrow

On Tastes, the Journey, and Clowning

by DANIELE FINZI PASCA

There is no inner path without guidance. And there
is no journey if, at times, you don't feel entirely lost.

To teach us to eat properly, my mother used to put books under
our armpits. The books had to stay firmly in place, without falling
onto the floor, while we cut up tomatoes or rolled spaghetti. This is
how my two brothers and I learned table manners. It wasn't meant
as a punishment but rather as a preparation for being able to enjoy
good food. It is a kind of wisdom that is still with me, even today.
Knowing how to behave at the table—to serve wine to the guests
first, wait until everyone is together before taking the first bite,
treat the food with delicacy, and enjoy the flavors—is something
that will really help you in life.

At Easter, my father would drive 300 kilometers to buy a special sweet bread made by special hands. The bakery would sell him the bread, and then he would drive 300 kilometers back, just so that we could all eat it together. Before the accident, Papa would do extravagant things like that—things that had a strong influence on me.

Whenever I try something new, I feel a peculiar kind of joy, as though each new taste is teaching me something new about the world and about myself. But, most of all, I find it fascinating to realize that a certain flavor will repeat itself—even with the passage of time. That's why I love going back to places where I have eaten in the past to verify that the tastes haven't changed, or rather that someone *has* changed something so that the taste remains the same. In fact, re-creating a flavor over the years requires a special kind of art. While she would knead gnocchi on a Sunday, my grandmother would say out loud, "To be sure that they're always the same, you need to make them a little bit different each time." And that is how I have conceived and created every show, song, and acrobatic stunt ever since: as though it were a dish of gnocchi that I am inviting everyone to share at my table.

Initiation in India

The first time I went to India, I stayed for six months. That was in 1983. A few days after I arrived, I spent three nights sleeping in the Benares train station. There was a young Indian boy with me. We had some eggs, a little salt, and a few coins. I was surrounded by the smells of the spices the local people ate. I learned to eat their hot spices. On the station floor we also had "table manners." But I got a stomach upset that left me flat out for nearly two days. Some flavors in life need more preparation than others. Your stomach doesn't always resist, but it does adapt.

I had left home convinced that by performing some of my clown routines I'd be able to help children and adults on whom life had turned its back. That was my intention when I arrived at the Shishu Bhavan children's center in Calcutta. The Missionaries of Charity usually don't allow men to work there. I insisted. I said that in addition to helping, I would do some clown gags. They agreed.

I prayed before taking the plunge and walking into that place. As it turned out, I never had time to give even the slightest thought to anything I had planned on doing. There was no space for putting on a red nose, no space to do any juggling or to get your shoes in a tangle, no space to pretend you were running behind a policeman who was chasing you. There was no space. There were no gloves. We didn't have any disinfectant. The first few days I covered my nose with a handkerchief.

In the very early morning, we would pick up the bodies of those who had died during the night. This would make room for new patients to be brought in. I was charged with going into the slums, because somehow I managed to find my way about in their labyrinthine alleyways. Then I would come back to the center with a sick child in my arms. I would moisten their lips, wash them, give them a bite to eat, comb their hair, and be there with them as they died. We communicated through our eyes and through our skin, so that they could pass away with someone beside them. That was all.

One day I brought in a little girl, folded in my arms. Her name was Sashi. She was six or seven years old and extremely weak. I was looking for a place to lay her down and wash her, but by the time I found somewhere, it was too late: she was dead. I stood there looking at her, still cradled in my arms. I simply couldn't understand how it could have happened so fast. Change of plan. Now that space was for the next person I needed to go and fetch. Sashi had gone. I didn't understand, but I had to go on working. I didn't understand a thing.

I also worked at the Kalighat center. When Sunil arrived there, the open wounds on his back were already infected. It was a question of minutes or maybe a few hours. He was somewhere between fifteen and twenty years old. I washed his wounds, and I remember cleaning small insects out of the cuts. Sister Luc said they had found him on the station floor. He was extremely thin. I cut his hair and stayed by his side. He looked at me. I took his hand. He didn't talk. Neither did I. The day passed. I went back the next day convinced that Sunil must have died during the night. But there he was, and he went on to survive for twenty-four days. No one could understand it. Sometimes life has that kind of tenacity. I learned a lot through Sunil's eyes, deep black and transparent. He died one day when I was not at the center. Our theater company carried his name for twenty-eight years.

I always had the impression that Guido, Atilio, Mother Teresa, and the missionary sisters knew that I wasn't going to be doing any clown stunts, but even so they let me work alongside them. During the journey of initiation that we all take at some point in our lives, teachers are essential and so is silence. To know how to guide is also to know how to keep quiet at times, or to say the right words. There is no inner path without guidance. And there is no journey if, at times, you don't feel entirely lost.

In the silence of the Eastern night, I recorded the things that happened to me on cassettes, for the family. That was the height of technology at the time: a small recorder. All day long I would tell myself about the day, so I would remember it and be able to tell others about it afterward. In the middle of that stifling heat, that persistent humidity, and the never-ending mosquitoes, I concentrated on trifles—minute details, perfumes, tiny things, little gestures given or received—all representing life while it was being lived.

That technique had a strong effect on the way I focused later on in my work as an actor. The imagination unfolds with open eyes, to narrate life *at exactly the same time* as you are living it. Everything is happening now, but when it is told it is already in the past, as though it comes from another time. This is a way in which you can prepare yourself better for empathy. To honor the teachers. To carry forward the tradition.

Are there schools that teach parents how to rock their child? No, what happens is that you observe, you see how it's done by the grandmother, by a lady who looks after babies, or by a friend who just caresses a spot on the baby's forehead. Then, suddenly, when the child is given to you, you don't know how to move it around. You sing to it, you pull it close to your heart, you walk with long steps, and gradually you start to get clues as to how to rock it. Our elders and our teachers communicate their experiences through example. It is such great good fortune to be able to meet them and learn from them. Even though you might end up transforming their legacy, still you are paying tribute to them.

· · ·

My vision of clowning changed radically after my time in India. I was nineteen years old when I returned home. With my brothers and a few close friends, we set about establishing a new kind of theater. We talked about a "new theatrical grammar," so that it would sound complicated and seem more intellectual, whereas in reality it was something that came from the gut. Our first meeting was at the Grotto Sant' Antonio in Balerna. We sat there together, enjoying our meal, and began jotting down the first ideas on a blank sheet of paper: shaking up the spectator, an introduction into the mystery, telling stories to heal, telling stories to make fear go away, training ourselves in our gestures to look the audience right in the eye, keeping an attentive awareness of everything going on round about, and staying aware of the effect of our actions.

Since that meeting many things have changed, but the intuitions remain. Just like my grandmother's gnocchi, each show has been a little bit different, to keep the flavor the same. You transform yourself so as to remain faithful to yourself as well.

In each performance of *Ícaro* I go back to the seed and return renewed by an inner journey. That's the place from which I face each new show. And everything always arises from around a table— from *Ícaro* to the Olympic ceremonies, via the Cirque du Soleil, the operas, and every new project. I create shows like I create dinners that I'm preparing for a few people—a few intimate friends. The fact that, with time, some of those creations have drawn in the masses and traveled around the globe surprises me and brings me joy. But I swear that I originally thought of them as just for a few guests.

In April 2010, my wife, Julie, pointed out that for a few weeks five shows were running simultaneously: while I was presenting *Ícaro* in Montreal, *Donka* was in Voronezh, *Nebbia* in Madrid, *Corteo* in Fukuoka, and *Rain* in Bogota. Performances were taking place in Canada, Russia, Spain, Japan, and Colombia, all on the same night, like threads connecting one side of the world to the other. You may be helping to weave them together, even if your intention in going to the theater was simply to woo the love of your life or honor the memory of one who is gone.

Closer to the Mystery

When I got sick with malaria in India, I began to suffer from hallucinations. Even before that, though, I would often sit for hours, contemplating the sky. I would look at the sky and ask myself questions like: Do horses dream? Why do big fishes have to eat smaller fishes? Why is there pain? And why . . . why are there mysteries? Why did you have to clip your wings when you could have escaped? Some of them are not really questions but more like prayers—private prayers. The sky in the East seemed to be the same one that I saw from my garden at home, yet at the same time it was different.

As a child I was an altar boy at the church around the corner from our home, the Sacred Heart. After meals, Papa always told us about the Jewish origins of the Finzi family. And in India, in the mountains that climb toward Nepal, I discovered Buddhism. Even today, when I first arrive somewhere, I look for the shamans. More than a question of religion, it is somehow linked to faith—one same heaven to which we pray in many different ways.

Once, I hung onto the belly of a lion: it was when a shaman at Mont-Tremblant near Montreal blindfolded me, stunned me with the beat of a drum, and introduced me to my animal guide. Clinging to the lion's belly, we followed a street that passed by the drain of the fountain in the garden of the house where I lived as a child—my home, from which you could see the bell tower of the Sacred Heart. Afterward we went down into the bowels of the earth where I met a lot of people, including Mister Puricelli, who was pumping up the tires of the bicycles of all the children in the neighborhood.

There are connections that bring you close to the mystery without betraying it. Because to speak about mystery you need a certain modesty, certain manners, something like those that our mother taught us while sitting at the table. You can't be distracted when you're in front of a ritual. I don't think the angels climbing up and down Jacob's Ladder push each other around: they ask politely and are grateful when another angel allows them to take their place and arrive more quickly.

My grandmother, the other one, not the gnocchi one, always said, "Never look at the floor. Even when you're sad, don't look down, always look up, to the sky. Because it's from up there that something good will come to you, for sure." In my shows, things are always raining down from above: water, shoes, petals, corks, *diabolos*, or letters.

Looking at the sky was where my fascination for rituals began, and it was the name of the first show after I came back from Calcutta. At the same time I tried to understand how the builders of cathedrals filled their constructions with references and clues. I became interested in the analysis of shapes and alchemical processes, things like the complexity of tarot cards or the alchemy needed to create a feast from a kilo of potatoes.

The nicest moment on a Sunday was being in the sacristy, when Father Reggiori would ask me to help him prepare the bread and the wine. A few minutes later, they would transform into body and blood. When I watched all this, I always wanted to discover the exact moment when the wine turned into blood. Actually the sacristy is similar to the proscenium, the space in front of the curtain in a theater. For me, it is the clown who specializes in being in the proscenium, that place which is neither stage nor stall, just as the sacristy is neither the altar nor the nave in the church. There are places that are a frontier and a threshold, like a quay or the foot of a sick person's bed.

In front of the curtain, the clown has a chance to look the public directly in the eye and induct them into the story. They have to believe you. It's not about truth or lies—it's about faith. It's about trust and the audience allowing itself to be carried along. This is why the clown is a guide and why as a clown you have to be attentive, because others are putting their trust *in you*. You must never fall into automatic behavior. Each night is different, and each spectator deserves for it to be like the very first time. We clowns repeat the movements so that each performance is different from the previous one. I learned the importance of this while cutting the nails of a sick man in Calcutta.

It wasn't a child, it was an old man who was close to dying. I thought it would be nice to cut his nails, so as to get him ready. So I took his feet in my hands and I began. Every time I cut a piece of nail, he made a strange movement with his body. After awhile I realized that he was starting to bleed beneath the nails. I felt bad. I was really upset because I realized that I was losing the *attentiveness* that was necessary, and I was starting to move in an automatic way. I did things: I took, I carried, I tidied, I cleaned . . . but everything was becoming automatic. I was not paying attention to the effect of my actions. And that is dangerous.

It's a warning I carry with me even today and that I share with all the artists I work with. A clown must be very vigilant on stage, concentrating not only on the gestures made but also on the effect those gestures produce in the people in front of you. You must train to be outside the action you are performing.

Lightness and Shadows

Not long after returning from India, my brother Marco, Maria Bonzanigo, and I christened our technique with the name "Theatre of Caress." Now a caress can be as heavy as a blow. It's only with strength and pressure that we can alleviate the contortions we all carry around on our backs. The lightness that we are looking for is imbued with both the weight of the world and the density of thought. We create so as to caress the viewers, to mobilize them, so that their eyes pour with rain. To prepare yourself for the point where everything comes together is the closest you can come to the mystery. The architecture that sustains us is invisible but dense, complex, and forceful. This is why *lightness* is so important. The deeper you look to go into the discourse, the more primordial simplicity becomes. I think lightness is one of the distinctive features of everyone who makes up this company. As companions on this journey for many years, whenever things get stormy, we prepare the table to sit down and eat, to converse and gently calm the waters. Nowadays the company includes people from sixteen countries. We are all united by the rigors of the work, while lightness is the natural state for us to communicate in—respect, as well.

One day when I was a child, I went out into the square with some of my neighborhood friends. We came up with the idea of throwing a couple of stones at a blackbird. Against all expectation, we managed to hit it. The bird tried to take off and escape, its spindly legs pushing against the dust, but it was unable to move forward or get off the ground. It couldn't do it. Seeing the bird like that changed my entire path through life, and it was the same for a couple of my friends. There's nothing more shameful than taking a life, and without reason. A stone is thrown and a pretty song is silenced forever. Blinking becomes impossible, and peace is betrayed.

As clowns we throw stones from the stage. But we should always be careful to aim into the void, never at the heart, and never at a person's soul. What we have to do is just point toward their shadows.

Spectators should have the feeling of being shaken, which is why we take aim at the representations they make of themselves. We are mirrors in which the spectators see themselves reflected, and we throw stones at those incorporeal images that can even shatter into a thousand pieces without anyone being injured. To manage to create an impact on the shadow—that is the meaning of poetry. To touch a heart you look at the handkerchief hidden in the trouser pocket or between the breasts where grandmothers tend to keep it, so as to have it as close as possible to their eyes. Traditionally speaking, everyone who was going to the theater used to carry a handkerchief. We point at that little piece of material because it represents the soul, and if there isn't a handkerchief we point at a wallet, a tie, a jacket left in the foyer.

Nor is it necessary to writhe around in pain on stage. Water, like rain, can fall from a person's eyes without destroying their soul. It's better the soul remain vigilant and attentive to what is happening among the spectators. Their tears should be real, ours should not.

Searching for Mushrooms

Writing a show is like collecting mushrooms: you have good days and you have bad days, mornings that are propitious and days when it's not even worth taking a stroll in the woods. You have to rise early, be the first to get there, know secret places, follow strokes of intuition, and know that close to one mushroom there's another, because like ideas, the good ones are never alone. To write, to create an acrobatic number or a poem, is like going in search of mushrooms. Not every one you find is good: just like ideas, some can spoil others and some can even poison you.

There is a tenderness in those who take a novice into the forest for the first time: "Come over here, look behind that pine tree . . ." You do everything you can to ensure the beginner stumbles across a mushroom that is out in the open. The novice approaches but does not see it, nearly crushes it. "Look carefully!" we insist . . . but it remains unseen. The truth is, it's a personal experience; you need to know what you're looking for before you can find the fragment you envision.

Before going on stage, I always cover my back with a jacket or a shawl. Mushrooms appear at the end of the summer and at the beginning of autumn, and when you leave the house early in the morning, it's a good idea to take something with you in case it gets cool in the afternoon. When I have to go on stage, it's as though I am preparing to take a walk in the woods, because all the stages the world over take on the hues of autumn just before the show begins.

Before a show, the technicians and the actors walk around the stage and the sets. They're looking for mushrooms, they're looking for the letters of the word "truth" to stick on the brow of the puppet they will become once the curtain rises. I slip on a jacket, because theaters also have an air of the harbor about them, and the billowing curtain resembles the sail of a ship. We clowns are at the prow, which is the proscenium, where sea spray splatters our faces. You need to have flexible knees, to be able to put up with the movement of the waves. In front of the wind-filled sail, you need to have free hands and a free heart. I abandon the jacket between the wings before reaching the prow.

The curtain is a sail. When you brush it, and when it begins to move, the forest transforms into the ocean, and looking for mushrooms changes into following whales and dancing with the dragon, which is the audience. If I lick my hands when I finish performing *Ícaro*, there is always a taste of salt on my tongue. Anyone who thinks it's perspiration is wrong; it's the taste of the ocean.

Writing is like fishing. A fisherman knows where to cast the line: studying the mirror of the sea and interpreting the currents in the water, he discovers the movement of the fish. He can remain motionless for hours, but he is working. Just like artists. There's a strange tendency to think that artists don't do anything. It's a mistake to think that we spend hours without working: we are hunters, fishermen, and mushroom collectors. Like chameleons, we can stay still for hours, waiting for an idea, an intuition, to pass by, close to our lips.

Sitting in front of a cup of coffee and a blank sheet of paper, I look out over the square. I don't move, I don't write anything, I wait, simply wait in silence. Then, suddenly there's a tug and I start to struggle with and reel in an idea that's swallowed the bait. A valuable fish may be worth days of motionlessness.

In India I cured myself by working. Actually I'm more disposed toward those egos that spill out into the world than to those who spend hour after hour in introspection. Lightness has to do with pouring that life out over others. And it has to do with caring for and cultivating that treasure known as friendship. Nearly all the stories I tell are a way of paying homage to friends.

Encouraging the Dawn

Ever since I was a child, I have always slept only a little—four hours a night, at times less. It's true, throughout the day I do take a few short naps—five or seven minutes are enough. I fall into dreamland with great ease. I'm filled with images, and when I wake up I remember them. During our rehearsal periods, I may sleep up to nine times during the course of the day; but the images for my shows rarely come entirely from dreams. In the dreamlike state, I look for elements that encourage the dawn—elements that reveal a new fold in reality. More than material for therapies or the unconscious, dreams are the place where facts are forged. The seed. The egg.

Once I was preparing Christmas dinner with Julie when the telephone rang. A friend from my brother Gabrielle's high school told me that a foundation was offering us an original backdrop by Salvador Dali to use in a show. For some weeks already, we'd been giving shape to an acrobatic show that would speak about truth. We accepted responsibility for the backdrop, and then there it was—an enormous piece measuring 15 meters by 9 meters on which Dali had painted a representation of Tristan and Isolde.

I approached Dali thinking that we shared a taste for sea urchins. We were united by a particular flavor, but we were divided in the way we interpreted dreams. Going in search of the pictures he painted when he was sick and old helped me sense certain bridges. That happened too when I was looking around his house near Cadaqués with Julie.

When I used to recite one of the passages in *Giacobbe*, I would sit on a wooden box, facing sideways toward the public. I laid great eggs there. But on the roof of Dali's house I also saw huge eggs. It was then that I understood that I had been tricked by the shape. For Dali, every object had a deep significance, alluded to and evoked by means of the language of symbols and dreams. I, however, am interested in eggs because the actors I have known have that strange and generous habit of leaving behind small and perfect signs of their passage, reminding me that to be a poet it may be necessary to know how to spit out precise and perfect gestures, fragile and rich—gestures and thoughts in the shape of an egg.

When we paid homage to Chekhov in *Donka*, the approach was crystalline. I remember traveling to Taganrog with Maria and hiding under the table where Chekhov ate as a child. We had to wait until all the museum guides had left, so as to be able to experience how things looked from underneath. It was on that same table that Chekhov had performed his first dissections of insects, for he was a man of the theater and of medicine. I believe most profoundly that something of Chekhov exists in the Russian spirit—which is what I sought to portray in the Opening Ceremony of the Sochi Paralympics in 2014. Chekhov created theater, he went fishing, and he cured sick people while his tuberculosis progressed and he kept it subtly hidden.

When I got malaria, along came the hallucinations, by which point I couldn't even dream. I couldn't think. I also got typhoid fever in India, as well as something like an allergic reaction to the monsoon rains. My hands and feet swelled up and broke out in sores, and I had an unbearable itchiness in my groin. Barely having returned to Lugano, I visited a dermatologist who was horrified to find me full of ticks as well. As a preventative measure, my whole family and a few friends too all followed a disinfection treatment.

Originally, *catharsis* was a medical term: to purge that which carried the discomfort and return the body to its normal functioning. Theater and medicine come from a common root. Time and time again we lose ourselves, get ill, and need to purify ourselves so as to be able to continue resisting. Illness and resistance are at the foundation of all the stories my clowns tell, those "loser heroes" whose small actions move the world forward.

Some time ago I met the father of an acquaintance of mine on a corner. It was years since I had seen him. I had grown up in the neighborhood, playing football with his son and going to the same school. He gave me a hug and said, with real joy, "It's lovely to see how well you've done, Daniele. I wouldn't have bet a single penny on you myself." In my mind I immediately remembered the day the teachers called my mother, concerned because I was still walking around in sandals and shorts despite the snow. My mother explained that I suffered from a particular kind of allergy to all types of wool. After that they no longer commented on my clothes. What my mother had said was a lie. There was no allergy. There was simply the wish to be different, to evade being normal.

My parents allowed us to develop that creativity, that untidy energy that makes you want to do things. I didn't want to be like the rest; I wanted to wear sandals in the snow; I wanted to be other than normal. In some villages this is particularly difficult, and no one wants to bet a penny on a kid like that. So you're really lucky if your family protects you from that kind of uniformity and allows your uniqueness to flower. A bottle of Ritalin would never have been allowed in our house. We paid attention to an infinity of things. Neighborhood friends would come to our house to play with us. It was a house with open doors.

Before the accident, Papa would spend hours in the darkroom developing photos. He had inherited his father's and his grandfather's trade. He allowed me to be in there with him. I remember it perfectly; I remember every movement and the prints hanging by small wooden pegs. The pictures would rise to the surface. Moments frozen in time. Evocative details. Everything in my house was about nostalgia—a journey back in time.

That atmosphere is what I try to recreate in my shows. Creating a show is my way of returning to Papa's darkroom, a way of thanking Mama for letting me wear sandals in winter. A way of honoring my grandmother's cooking.

MY LETTER TO HUMANITY

What I would really love to do is to talk to those who have left us and gone. For years, I had them there, right next to me, and it did not seem possible that one day they would disappear. So I like to think about them now, because when I try to remember them, there is less danger of my forgetting the people who loved me. They are my guides, my pole star, the flavors and scents that lead me home. And me, I am a clown. My job is telling stories about "loser heroes"—heroes who almost always lose out.

Those who have already departed have left me their legacy: all kinds of stories for getting rid of fear. For fear is worse than pain. It traps us in a corner, it paralyzes us, it makes us catch our breath, and then we struggle for air and cannot think with any poise or calmness. But there are certain tales that can help us overcome fear, strengthen our courage, and help us win back our equanimity. And as clowns, our whole business is passing on these stories that shamans, visionaries, and our very own grandmothers knew how to make up.

I would love to think for a while about friends, too. Friendship is a bond that is magical and inexplicable. Lost as it were in time, it can push us forward and take us back home, all in the single moment of a hug or an embrace. Almost all the stories that I have written are to do with friendship. When someone calls me "brother" to show me his love, I understand what he wants to tell me, and I am grateful. Yet what I find even more extraordinary is when you can say about a brother that he is also your friend. To be all sons of the same father or mother is beautiful enough, but to be connected with a person for magical reasons like the ties created by friendship is something that is extraordinarily precious. Friendship is a secret and mysterious force, and lucky are those who have known this uncanny experience.

I would love to understand what empathy is, just so that I could talk about it. How can you train yourself not to slip into indifference when you encounter somebody else's suffering? How does it work, this strange reaction that makes us feel close, present, and ready to take a complete stranger in our arms? This impulse, this energy that makes us cross the road, change direction, choose a different way of life—where does it come from? If we knew how empathy worked, I would look for a way to train in it, and I would season my stories with its spice.

I would love to know how to build containers for happiness. The thing is that we all have a share of happiness available to us in life. There are those dawns and sunsets that we are too lazy to walk out into the garden to enjoy, and so we lose them forever. There are those star-filled nights, meetings with people, silences, parties, fragrances, and flavors that we are in danger of wasting. There are those occasions, and every life has its share, that are just made for taking someone in your arms and dancing. I know happiness cannot be preserved in a jar, but I know some people who are able to become an orchestra. Like them, we too have the power to transform ourselves into musical instruments capable of letting loose a tempest of sound, of aching melodies that can fill us with inspiration and invite us simply to lose ourselves for a second in a dizzying whirl, and to dance, for dance is the simplest pathway to happiness, the simplest of all.

I would love it if we managed at least once a week to sing a song all together, the same one, at the same moment, and from one end of the planet to the other. There are some words that are just too difficult—"humanity" is too big for me; I can't see the edges of such a gigantic enterprise. In my job, I have discovered that choral singing is a beautiful way of losing yourself in a group, where you blend into one voice, deeply united and unique. In chorus, our aim is to create beauty together, and then that beauty wafts its flavors and scents everywhere, all around—just for a short while, for the duration of one song.

So this is what would make me happy: the extent to which we succeeded in singing at least one song a week all together, making use of all the talent we have in our hearts, telling stories that conquer fear, honoring those who have gone by telling their stories, holding ourselves close, and holding ourselves in one another's arms for just a few moments—the length of a song, a dance, a thunderstorm, or a sunset—or as long as it takes to bake a loaf of focaccia.

Then, after the stories, music, songs, and poems, there will be silence as well, an entire space we need to live in with a certain lightness. It is the space that belongs to those who have beaten fear and who can lose themselves, forget all about certainties, and discover brand new pathways. Silence is like the whiteness of a blank page that is waiting to be written on. I wish for myself, I wish for all of us, that a child will appear who can find a new way to write down the ideas that will change humanity, new ideas that will satisfy all our desires for justice and peace. I wish this blank page could, for a brief instant, gather together the visions that will fire us off toward new horizons.

We clowns, we dance and we sing to banish fear so that the visionaries can settle serenely into that silence and that vast space that lies empty and waiting to be filled with new ideas, with poetry and justice. We are all loser heroes. We are all clowns. We are all entrusted with the secrets and the hopes that make fear go away. We are all responsible for those blank pages that someone, one of these days, will fill with the right ideas.

—Daniele

Putting Our Heart
into the World

by PATRICK GAFFNEY

By fusing creativity and compassion, we can step
beyond the ordinary, transcend narrow self-interests,
teach ourselves a new habit of other-centeredness,
and find a vivid sense of purpose.

You might easily say, "Well, all the stories and letters I have just read concerned special people. Of course they made an impact, because they were all so talented. It's easy to do great things and change the world if you are someone with all kinds of skills and abilities from the beginning. But what can I do?"

None of the individuals we met in this book, were they asked, would claim to be exceptional. Perhaps, at the most, they might admit that they were ordinary people who led extraordinary lives. Or they might say that their lives were made remarkable by virtue of their connection to other people. In any case, their stories portray the power of transformation and the extraordinary richness of humanity, which is what makes them so compelling and so moving. Our storytellers discovered how to fuse together two fundamental and most human qualities, imagination and compassion, and in so doing, they helped countless men, women, and children and opened a door. Or left it ajar. For people like us.

But how can we achieve anything like them? They would be the first to grab us by the sleeve and tell us that human beings *all*—each and every one—possess a wealth of talents and creativity. They would tell us not to get stuck on some limiting notions and stereotypes of what talent and aptitude might be. They would tell us that we must never believe we have to be a famous personality, or an accomplished artist, or belong to some creative elite before we can do things that change the lives of others for the better or create a kinder and more merciful world. We do not have to make ourselves special; we already are.

Being Human

So what is it that can provoke us to change our lives and make changes in the world? Many people say that the single most important thing that gives purpose and meaning to our life is our deep connection with other human beings. And here we are, seven billion of us and counting. Dr. Martin Luther King Jr. said: "We are caught in an inescapable network of mutuality, tied in a single garment of destiny. Whatever affects one directly, affects all indirectly. This is the interrelated structure of all reality."

All of us are profoundly connected to one another. Aren't we all descended from one lady in East Africa? We are all making our way through our lives, just like one another, with the same goal—that is to find fulfillment and meaning and avoid pain and anxiety. What this means is that our happiness and others' happiness are forever interwoven, as Dr. King expressed so movingly in his vision of the whole human family moving forward together: "You can never be what you ought to be until I become what I ought to be. By the same token, though, I can never become what I ought to be until you become what you ought to be."

Two of the greatest characteristics we have as human beings are imagination and empathy, which run like a vein of gold through the lives of the individuals in this book. *Empathy*, that instinct in the blood, that capacity we have to feel and in some ways participate in the experience of others, whether joy or sorrow, is the ground of compassion. Daniele calls it "this impulse, this energy that makes us cross the road, change direction, choose a different way of life." And because we have *imagination*, not only can we have a vision of the future, but we can also see and feel what it is like to stand in someone else's shoes.

We all have that seed of compassion within us, as part of our human nature. This is who we are. Not only do the ancient contemplative traditions tell us this, but Charles Darwin also maintained that *sympathy*—which today would include compassion—is the strongest of our human instincts, and he imagined it expanding to embrace "all sentient beings." One of today's leading primatologists, reflecting on the origins of human nature, says, "Compassion is not a recent weakness going against the grain of nature, but a formidable power that is as much a part of who and what we are as the competitive tendencies it seeks to overcome."[1]

But what exactly is compassion, which we hear about so often these days and which is the underlying message of all the stories in this book? Here is one beautiful description: "Not simply a sense of sympathy or caring for the person suffering, not simply a warmth of heart toward the person before you, or a sharp clarity of recognition of their needs and pain, it is also a sustained and practical determination to do whatever is possible and necessary to help alleviate their suffering. Compassion is not true compassion unless it is active."[2]

Simply put, compassion is the desire to relieve suffering and its causes, coupled with an urge to do something about it. Compassion has sometimes been called "the inability to bear someone else's suffering."

It is all-embracing: you can throw in love, tolerance, respect, forgiveness, patience, inclusiveness, kindness, and joy as well, and they all make up compassion. It has nothing to do with pity or condescension and everything to do with treating others just as we would want to be treated ourselves. But what is barely understood, and yet so vital for our future, is that we can actually *cultivate* compassion, by bringing together our natural feelings of empathy with our imagination, reason, and will.

How is that possible? One of the first steps in cultivating compassion is to try to look honestly at the world through another person's eyes. Experience that person's craving for happiness and freedom, his or her fear of suffering and pain, with the same immediacy that we would feel if we were that individual. Maybe their hopes or their fears are even greater or more paralyzing than our own. Putting ourselves in someone else's shoes, we can feel the ground on which they stand. This simple but eye-opening exercise is vital for understanding compassion.

If it is human nature to be compassionate, then why is the world like it is? Why is it so difficult for us to think and act out of altruism and not out of self-interest? In asking this question, we are putting our finger on the very thing that is the number-one cause of all our frustration, suffering, and confusion. It's that we have no idea of who we really are. We spend our whole lives confined to a claustrophobic bubble world, putting ourselves first, and seeing everything through the lens of our self-centeredness. We all want to be special, to be creative, to be original, to be the best—to be celebrities in fact.

What is the price of this self-centeredness? No secrets here. Inevitably, it can only narrow down our vision, aggravate our suffering and self-pity, rob us of contentment, incline us to blame others and dodge responsibility, and turn our tiniest misfortune into catastrophe. We all know what this feels like. It's a habit. And this self-fixation, when magnified onto a greater stage of the economy or the environment, is absolutely disastrous.

This is why to think of others or take time to train our minds and hearts in compassion is a dramatic change. It naturally expands our minds and makes them more spacious, because we need to fit more people in. The feeling that we are the only ones in the whole world to suffer and that our problems are so immense and unmanageable begins to slip away. Compassion means staying present in the face of suffering, whether ours or someone else's, and so it gives us inner strength, confidence, courage, and fearlessness. That courage arms us with resilience, so that we can accept and deal with anything that comes along. All in all, what we discover is that the huge quantity of energy we have locked up in protecting, pampering, and solidifying the self is set free to enable us to stay focused and undistracted in the present moment or to help others.

Despite all of this, we might still question thinking about others and steeping ourselves in compassion. Isn't it just a burden, one more thing on the list in our crowded, preoccupied lives? What is truly miraculous, and has been shown by recent research and scientific studies, is that if we make a habit of thinking, feeling, or acting with compassion, it brings *us* an astounding range of benefits. It seems that training in compassion can make us less stressed, healthier, more successful in our personal and work relationships, and of course more kind, as well as boosting our immune system.

Volunteering, for example, is shown to improve morale, self-worth, positive feelings and well-being, lead to a longer life, and decrease symptoms of depression. It appears that a genuine feeling of concern for others looks after our own physical and mental well-being as a matter of course, whatever its benefit for others. One psychologist says,

> Strange perhaps, and paradoxical, but true. The most sensible way to further *our own* interests, to find *our own* freedom, and to glimpse *our own* happiness, is often not to pursue these goals directly, but to look after *other* people's interests, to help *other* people be freer from fear and pain, to contribute to *their* happiness. Ultimately, it is all very simple. There is no choice between being kind to others and being kind to ourselves. It is the same thing.[3]

Reza reminds us of the poet Saadi and his words "Human beings are all the limbs of one body." This betrays the vast and universal sweep of compassion. There is only one single difference between others and us: they outnumber us, seven billion to one. All of us need one another. Genuine love and compassion do not depend on another person's *attitude* or *behavior* or *relationship* toward us; they depend simply, nakedly, on the fact that other people exist and breathe and laugh and suffer and die in front of us. Warm-heartedness is something we can generate for everyone, based on the mere fact of their *being* alive, as human beings.

Defining Our Best Self

Our storytellers in this book, Reza, Bob and Sherry, Aliza, Deeyah, Yarrow, and Daniele all found a glorious purpose in their lives. It's often said that the one characteristic that defines human beings is their search for meaning. Don't we often have that sense that there is something missing, something tantalizingly close, that nagging suspicion that we are not attending to the most important thing in life? For many years, researchers have investigated what makes work meaningful, interviewing employees in different industries, who said that the greatest source of meaning came from believing that their jobs had a positive impact on other people, brought them benefit, and contributed to society. And the research showed that having purpose and meaning in life increases overall well-being and life satisfaction, improves mental and physical health, reinforces resilience, enhances self-worth, and decreases the chances of depression.

How is this possible? After witnessing and enduring unimaginable suffering in concentration camps during the Second World War, the psychiatrist and neurologist, Viktor Frankl, wrote his epic book, *Man's Search for Meaning*. He said:

> Being human always points, and is directed, to something or someone, other than oneself—be it a meaning to fulfill or another human being to encounter. The more one forgets himself—by giving himself to a cause to serve or another person to love—the more human he is.[4]

Often we limit or belittle ourselves by underestimating who we are as human beings. We cannot seem to see who we really are. The French writer Albert Camus said: "Man is the only creature who refuses to be what he is." We are so much bigger than we think. The truth may be—for it is up to us to confirm it—that we all have a limitless treasure of love, of compassion, of power, of practical wisdom inside of us.

Yarrow tells us, "The moment you define your better self, the closer you are to becoming it." Why not declare it and celebrate it? We have an infinite sky-like mind and a heart as big as the world, full of boundless compassion and love. Why not face the truth of who we are as human beings and stand in awe, rather than perpetuate the mediocre, sepia-toned version of ourselves?

To have a bigger vision of ourselves as human beings, to recognize who we really are, is a transformation. What was always there, but hidden, is revealed. What was not seen is seen, and what we could not dream of we can now imagine. Because it is our imagination that limits how we see ourselves and others and how we can, in even small ways, change the world. By fusing creativity and compassion, we can step beyond the ordinary, transcend narrow self-interests, teach ourselves a new habit of other-centeredness, and find a vivid sense of purpose.

Paying Attention to an Infinity of Things

As Reza, Sherry, Bob, Aliza, Deeyah, Yarrow, and Daniele tell their stories, what is striking is that the experience that changed their lives was triggered by an encounter of some kind that seemed perfectly ordinary but had a sublime consequence: the old lady in the fish market, the teenage musical genius condemned to prison, the young Muslim woman behind the counter in the post office, a book on spirituality dating back to 1971, the childhood tormentor forgiven and seen as a teacher, or a dying youth in India who had so much to give. These seemingly random incidents became, innocently, the catalysts for transforming our friends, and through them, countless others.

Even great things can have their origins in the simplest event or a meeting with one other human being. As a young woman in her twenties, Cicely Saunders took up nursing in London when the Second World War broke out. Qualifying as a medical social worker, at St Thomas' Hospital in 1948 she met and became very close to a forty-year-old Polish man called David Tasma, who had escaped the Warsaw ghetto and worked in London as a waiter. He was suffering from an inoperable cancer. They spent a lot of time together as he came closer to death. And as they talked, what actually materialized was her mission in life, and at the same time a vision—a vision of a place designed to bring dignity and humanity to those who were dying and their families. When he died, David Tasma left her a gift of £500, to be, he said, "a window in your home." Cicely Saunders devoted the rest of her life to caring for the dying, and in 1967, she opened that home,

St. Christopher's Hospice, the first modern hospice in the world, and went on to inspire the spread of hospices and a complete transformation in palliative care in many places. Yet she insisted, "I didn't set out to change the world; I set out to do something about pain."[5]

In 1966, the young Buddhist nun Cheng Yen was visiting a medical clinic in her native Taiwan and caught sight of a pool of blood on the floor. She was told that it came from a local woman who was suffering from complications when she had gone into labor. Her family had carried her down from their mountain village, an eight hours' walk, but could not afford the hospital fees and had to carry her back, untreated. Cheng Yen was distraught, overwhelmed with sadness at the cruel fate of this unknown woman, and there and then she determined to build a hospital for the poor. So she founded the Tsu Chi Foundation that today works in seventy-two countries, in the fields of medicine, education, and disaster relief, with thousands of volunteers serving all over the world. And Tsu Chi has built not one, but several, hospitals.[6]

Will such important moments or meetings ever occur in our lives too? Maybe they already do. Perhaps, Reza or Daniele would tell us, we will encounter our old lady or our dying youth any day now, if we have not done so already. But what is it that turns an ordinary event into a crucial and powerful moment of transformation? Are the individuals who experience it in some particularly vulnerable or receptive state? Or maneuvered by life into a place where they are unable to miss the signs the world is giving them? Or is it simply their curiosity to discover, their fascination for life?

In each case those people are able, and ready, to recognize something in what is unfolding in front of them, and through that awareness their humanity touches the humanity of others, and unknowingly gazes through the mirror into the hearts of millions. They recognize this then or later as a seminal moment. Yet how do they do that? By being present, being awake, and being aware of others.

So our task may be to learn how to take notice and pay attention to the ordinary magic of small things, to train our heart to follow the score that the world is playing, or for a moment to see this very world as a screen on which messages are being relayed, furnishing us with all kinds of clues and hints. Can we remain intrigued and enchanted and keep our curiosity alive? It is as if we become a team member, working hand in hand with the universe. Daniele told us "we paid attention to an infinity of things." The poet Rilke captured it: "Be alert for any sign of beauty or grace. Offer up every joy, be awake at all moments to the news that is arriving out of silence."

It seems that if there are doors that open up to us in life, only we can open our door and step through it; only we can choose the person to help us go forward. But we can only open a door if we see one there; we have to be aware enough to recognize, which means we have to notice and pay attention. So often we are lost in distraction, ruminating about the past or fretting about the future. How important it is, we can see, to reclaim the present moment, focus our awareness, and pay attention just to what is happening in front of us.

Of course this is another reason why we find it difficult to be compassionate; we simply do not notice. But every day we are surrounded by so many sights that can evoke compassion, so many chances to open our hearts, if we can only take them. The young man with his infant son on his shoulders trying to steer his way through the traffic and cross the street in the rain, that old lady with swollen legs laden down with plastic shopping bags and jostled by the crowd, the homeless person sitting on the ground with his starving dog unceasingly accosting people and yet ignored . . . and then there is the television with its hourly procession of tragedies from all over the world.

Whenever, wherever we feel compassion arising, at that moment, without brushing it aside, we can focus on it, go deep inside, and let our hearts open spontaneously, longing for that suffering to be eased and eliminated altogether. That *wish* is the crucially important factor, because it shapes our mind and creates a habit, but it does not mean that we shy away from *doing* something active to help or prevent injustice whenever we can.

The stories in this book have much to show us about change and transformation. But when we talk about transformation, we are not talking necessarily about profound spiritual transformation or enlightenment as in the great spiritual traditions of the world. We are talking about the day-to-day honest and grounded recognition of who we really are and who we can be, which is a transformation in itself.

There is another kind of transformation where we can consciously use the very experiences of our life as a training in compassion. Every fit of fury, bout of frustration, or petty jealousy, every time we want to bite someone's head off, we have in our hands a passport to understanding the troubles of thousands all over the world. Whenever we feel rage or fear or loneliness or betrayal, have just lost a loved one, or suffer from sickness or even are in the process of dying, we can make an immediate connection with the rest of humanity. It is as if, as a poet once said, we contain multitudes.

We already know that as human beings we all have a vast amount in common. Now we can take that knowledge of our shared humanity and use our imagination to go even deeper, to see if we can put ourselves *completely* in someone else's shoes. In the contemplative method called "giving and taking," whenever anything undesirable or painful happens to us, or any difficult feelings erupt, we breathe these in and at the same time arouse a heartfelt compassion for the countless people who are now undergoing the very same isolation or feeling the same pain or fear. And as we do so, we wish and we long for them to be free from it all. We breathe out relief, and space, and the capacity for them to live with greater ease with whatever pain they have to endure. In fact we send them whatever they need to be happy and well. We are already suffering, so why not give it meaning? Why not let our pain and anguish be enough to relieve the suffering of all those others in the world? And what we discover is that our hearts have no limits and are as vast as space. What we normally fear and run away from is transformed by the alchemy of compassion into the very raw material that will in one stroke begin to open our hearts and set us free from our self-preoccupation.

Transformation can also happen when we least expect it. Sometimes we give ourselves impossible standards to live up to, telling ourselves we have to become modern-day saints or climb mountains of one sort or another in order to prove ourselves. Instead, why not simply be ready and willing for ordinary things, events, and movements—the fluttering of a flag, the glancing shaft of sunlight through a window, a note of music, or the unstudied expression on a person's face—to release the magic and the passion of life in small episodes that can unfasten our hearts and spark a shift in consciousness, an intimation of some deeper dimension to things, and make us the helpless witness to perfection? This may not seem so rational or logical, and it is not such an explicit kind of transformation. It's more just a question of seeing what is not always seen, being inspired and moved to recognize the "news" that the world is constantly providing us, and drinking in these invisible parables and flashes of wonder that can, if we let them, be life changing.

Yet all of this depends on our being aware. All too often our lives are spent in the non-present, barely noticing what is happening. To come back to the present moment is indeed always a transformation.

It Just Takes a Spark

Looking at our world, one thing that stands out with inescapable clarity is that unless we evolve beyond the "us and them" mentality, unless we develop a genuine concern and warm-heartedness toward one another, and unless we link our imagination to empathy and compassion, there may be no future for our species on the planet. Scientists speak of a radical change in behavior required to avert a global catastrophe; this means huge changes, both personal and for society. The Kenyan Nobel laureate Wangari Maathai has given us this warning:

> In the course of history, there comes a time when humanity is called to shift to a new level of consciousness, to reach a higher moral ground. A time when we have to shed our fear and give hope to each other. That time is now.[7]

Looking at the global situation, the Canadian educationalist Brian K. Murphy concluded:

> We hold billions prisoner to the limits of our psychology and imagination, and seal the fate of humankind, because, quite literally, it is only through our own radical transformation . . . that a fundamental transformation of the conditions of all humankind can begin. This is our challenge. The choice is ours and only ours . . . and above all, that decision is, and can only be, a solitary, individual decision: to live, to choose, to act . . . [8]

This kind of transformation is what the men and women in this book, each in their own way, have discovered, fought for, and embodied. They have each championed values and principles that are desperately needed today: education, gender equality, compassion, freedom of speech, creativity, and peaceful coexistence. They show us, above all, that it *is* possible. They tell us that we *all* have the power to change the world, in all kinds of ways, however simple or modest. We don't need to be great professors, painters, poets, or movie directors. We have all the talent we need in the creativity of our own imagination and in the compassion of our hands and hearts.

But sometimes it all seems daunting and insurmountable, when we are juggling overpopulation, food shortages, poverty, pollution, financial debt, and climate change as well. What effect can we have, as just one person? That's when we need to remember this famous story:

A man is walking along the seashore one day as the tide ebbs, revealing a multitude of stranded starfish. Soon he comes upon a young girl picking up the starfish one by one and returning them to the sea. So he asks the girl, "What are you doing?"

And she replies, "They will die if I don't get them back into the water."

"But there are so many of them," the man says. "How can anything you do make a difference?"

The girl picks up another starfish and carries it to the sea. "It makes a difference to this one."[9]

There is no question: our presence here on earth indeed has a purpose and a meaning, because we can change the world. Sherry and Bob say, "It all begins with a vision of the future. Once you can envision a change, you are already halfway there." Yarrow tells us if we can believe, then we can see, and Deeyah sees a future nurtured by love, freedom, and equality. Vision calls us to be part of something much bigger than ourselves. Reza even pleads with us to imagine and to dream of a seed that germinates, sprouts, and blossoms into a giant tree of peace.

So we begin with a vision, our hope and dream, that positive effect we long to have on the world, but then we have to take the right action. We start with small steps and go forward one step after another, making a ripple in the sea of humanity. But we have to do *something*. The Irish statesman and thinker Edmund Burke warned, "Nobody made a greater mistake than he who did nothing because he could only do a little." Don't ever underestimate any benevolent or compassionate actions, however seemingly small or unglamorous. Didn't Yarrow's Superdudes include people who walked dogs, visited the elderly, and cleaned up parks? One day the Vietnamese monk and human rights activist Thich Nhat Hanh was asked by his student: "There are so many urgent problems, what should I do?" He replied, "Take one thing and do it very deeply and carefully, and you will be doing everything at the same time."[10]

If we are unsure about how to choose or what to contribute, then we can start by drawing up a list of our preoccupations and the issues that we feel passionate about or that are unjust or heartbreaking, and then brainstorm ideas and choose a priority. Of course, there are so many resources we can use like websites, libraries, and community centers.

In any case, we will need commitment, and we will need to tell ourselves that we *will* succeed and feel confident that we *can* contribute. Aristotle said that people learn how to be brave by doing brave things. We also need to have the courage to be imperfect. We will have to persevere and be persistent; just as Aliza found, "It took several years of trial and error, but I finally understood how to go about it." And as Sherry and Bob say, "It just takes a spark . . . Find your path, discover the talents and creativity we *all* possess within us. Put your heart into the world. The world needs you."

As these stories have shown, at the same time as we need vision, we also have to pay attention to the small details. We cannot get befuddled in grand abstract visions and become a "telescopic philanthropist," ignoring those around us. As much as we aspire to have compassion for all humanity, we have to show kindness to the people closest to us in our lives, and even the most difficult ones. Daniele cautions us: "I realized I was losing the attention that was necessary and I was starting to act more in an automatic way. I was not paying attention to the effects of my actions." The English visionary William Blake wrote: "He who would do good to another must do it in Minute Particulars."

The life stories in this book offer us so many extraordinary insights, guidelines, and ideas. For example, why not go out like Daniele one day and sit quietly and contemplate the sky? Why not treat every day and night as though they are something new? Why not keep a mind where there are open questions and space for uncertainty? Why do we need to make everything so solid and excruciating? Remember, lightness is vital, and so are humor and impishness, too. Being a human being is a messy business. Albert Einstein is supposed to have said, "Only two things are infinite, the universe and human stupidity, and I'm not sure about the universe."

A Million New Friends

Einstein is also believed to have said, "Only a life lived for others is a life worthwhile." That will do as the theme of this book. Let's hope that the stories in these pages inspire and motivate many, many people and that they find their way into schools and educational institutions of all kinds. How wonderful it would be if individuals in every part of the world, and especially children and young people, knew about these seven people and their work. We need more and more people like them, in fact, working as channels of social change and liberation at every level and in every situation of society.

The Dalai Lama put it like this:

> If you become a compassionate person, then your life will become meaningful. You will be content, calm and peaceful, and so your friends, or even the animals around you, will also be at peace. Then,

when it comes to *the last day of your life*, you will feel happy, knowing you have spent your life cultivating friendliness and peace. Really, you will feel happy. Otherwise, even if you're a billionaire, at that moment neither your money nor anything else will be of any use. And however beautiful your body, you have to leave everything behind. If your life has been one of compassion, then at that final moment, I think you will experience genuine satisfaction, and feel no regret. After all, the whole purpose of our life is to lead a happy and meaningful life. And in order to give it that meaning, ultimately warm-heartedness is the key.[11]

So Reza, Bob, Sherry, Aliza, Deeyah, Yarrow, and Daniele would tell us, in a chorus: don't ever think you don't count or you don't have it in you to change yourself and the world. Every single one of us can contribute, like the drops of water that become the stream that swells into a huge river and then dissolves into the ocean. Maybe that great Persian poet Hafiz puts it best:

I used to know my name. Now I don't. I think a river
understands me.
For what does it call itself in that blessed moment when
it starts emptying into the Infinite Luminous Sea,
and opening every aspect of self wider than it ever
thought possible?

Each drop of itself now running to embrace and unite
with a million new friends.
And you were there, in my union with All,
everyone who will ever see this page.[12]

There were six stories in this book, but now they all converge in the person seeing this page and reading these words. That means that the final story, if you accept, can be yours.

The next pages are left blank as an invitation to you, if you so wish, to compose your own *Letter to Humanity*, just as our seven friends have done. How would you put into words your wishes for the world and your aspiration to do something to bring change and make use of the talent that we all have in our hearts? Write whatever you like to the rest of your human family. And imagine "a million new friends" just waiting now to hear from you. If you like, share your deepest hopes and yearnings. Feel free to reveal your insights— and don't forget some thoughts about what you are going to do.

MY LETTER TO HUMANITY

Would you like to share your words and vision with "a million new friends"? We encourage you to upload your Letter to Humanity on our website: www.talentforhumanity.org

A NOTE FROM THE EDITOR

Thank you for reading this book, and thank you for writing your letter. And if you have been inspired or moved by these stories, let's never stop imagining. Let us join a conspiracy of compassionate action and sign up to a lineage of kindness that we can pass on forever. Let's believe we can evolve into a new brand of human beings, human beings that live for one another.

BIOGRAPHIES AND

FURTHER INFORMATION

REZA

A philanthropist, idealist, humanitarian, and architect by training, Reza is a world-famous photojournalist. He was born in Tabriz in Iran. For the past thirty years he has traveled the world bearing witness to war and peace, and in more than a hundred countries he has photographed conflicts, revolutions, and human catastrophes, as well as the beauty of humanity. His images appear in the international media like *National Geographic, Time, Stern, Newsweek, El Pais, Paris Match, Geo,* as well as in the books, exhibitions, and documentaries created by his agency, Webistan.

Reza is not just a photographer. Since 1983, he has been committed to training women and children around the world, to help them strive for a better life. In 2001, he founded the NGO "Aina in Afghanistan," a project dedicated to children's education and to the training of Afghan women in visual media and communication. Reza continues to lead photographic training programs, from refugee camps in war-ravaged regions to the European suburbs, while also producing incredible images from his travels.

Reza's exhibitions have included *Memories of Exile* at the Carrousel du Louvre in 1998, *Crossing Destinies* on the gates of the Luxembourg Gardens in Paris in 2003, *War + Peace* at the Caen Memorial Museum in Normandy in 2009, *One World, One Tribe* in many cities throughout the world in 2010, and *Hope,* the grand retrospective of his work in Doha, Qatar in 2012. Reza created *Soul of Coffee* in 2013, which pays tribute to the women and men coffee growers of India, Colombia, Brazil, Guatemala, Ethiopia, and South Sudan.

The author of twenty-seven award-winning books and fellow of the National Geographic Society, Reza has received many awards, including the World Press Photo award and the Infinity Award from the International Center of Photography as well as distinctions from several American universities. In 2005 the president of France awarded him the highest civilian honor, the Medal of Chevalier of the National Order of Merit.

Reza continues to capture and bear witness to the turmoil occurring around the world. "The world is my field of vision," he says. "From war to peace, like the ineffable moments of poetry, my photographs are intended to be testimonies of our humanity on the roads of life."

www.webistan.com

SHERRY AND BOB JASON

In 1977, new Public Defender Sherry Jason, taking her first tour of Central Juvenile Hall, met a boy having his first piano lesson. A prodigy, playing Mozart by ear, he was thirteen years old, incarcerated for murder, and awaiting placement in the California Youth Authority, a prison for youthful offenders. Sherry walked away wondering what this young man's case history would have been if he had met the piano and Mozart before he met guns and gangs.

Over the next five years, former-ballerina-turned-criminal-defense-attorney Sherry Jason and her husband Bob, also a Los Angeles County public defender, became convinced that utilizing the arts in prevention is crucial to solving the devastating problems of delinquency, crime, and violence.

In 1982, the Jasons began renovating what would become the City Hearts studio with money donated from their family, Bob's entire retirement fund, and other personal loans. Established as a nonprofit organization in 1984, City Hearts was founded on the belief that the arts are the most powerful tools to communicate with and rehabilitate troubled youth at risk from gangs and drugs.

Thirty years and 35,000 children later, "City Hearts: Kids Say Yes to the Arts" continues to create and implement innovative programs that help children grow and heal through the magic of the arts. Working with 2,500 children aged five–eighteen each year, City Hearts has come to be an integral part of the preventive and rehabilitative effort in Los Angeles and the inner city, and it serves as a model for youth programs across the country.

The goal of all City Hearts programs is to change lives by inspiring young hearts to nurture and cultivate the arts, and so to enable our community's most impoverished children to get involved in learning, recognize their value as creative contributors to society, and dream of a brighter future for themselves and their community. In Sherry Jason's words, "I always wanted the world to be a better place. And that's what I see in City Hearts: our attempt to make the world a better place through the arts, one child at a time."

www.cityhearts.org

ALIZA HAVA

Acclaimed as a captivating performer, Aliza Hava is a singer and songwriter whose introspective lyrics explore the deepest levels of love, life, spirituality, and the importance of positive social change. Her debut album, *RISE*, is a blend of classic rock, acoustic guitar, and soul influence. Released on her indie label, FireMusicFaerie Productions, *RISE* is an artistic statement of conscience calling for an end to war, a greater awareness of our collective environmental responsibilities, and respect for the unity of humanity.

Tracks from *RISE* have been heard on independent radio stations throughout the United States and overseas, including "All for Peace Radio" in Israel/Palestine, where Aliza works with various groups promoting peaceful coexistence.

She is the founder of several initiatives utilizing music as a tool for peace building, including *Harmony in the Holy Land*, a sacred music event creating peace through the healing power of music. Her performances have taken her across the United States to Australia, India, Latin America, the Far East, and the Middle East.

Aliza has appeared at Madison Square Garden, the Apollo Theater, Mountain Jam, New Orleans' House of Blues, and music festivals internationally. She has shared the stage with celebrated artists such as Michael Franti, Dr. John, Derek Trucks, Matisyahu, Tab Benoit & the Voice of the Wetlands, Jefferson Starship, Kevin Costner & Modern West, and Woodstock legend Richie Havens.

Her original songs feature alongside Annie Lenox and Rickie Lee Jones on the soundtrack of the award-winning documentary *FEMME: Women Healing the World*. Directed by Emmanuel Itier and produced by Sharon Stone, *FEMME* features Nobel laureates and prominent female leaders, teachers, and artists who use their gifts to help create a better world.

www.alizahava.com

DEEYAH KHAN

Deeyah Khan is a critically acclaimed music producer and Emmy and Peabody award-winning documentary film director whose work highlights human rights, women's voices, and freedom of expression.

Her skill as a multidisciplinary artist led her to use music and film as the language for her social activism. Born in Norway to immigrant parents of Pashtun and Punjabi ancestry, the experience of living between different cultures—both the beauty and the challenges—dominates her artistic vision.

Her 2012 film *Banaz: A Love Story* won several international awards. This documentary chronicles the life and death of Banaz Mahmod, a young British Kurdish woman killed in 2006 in London on the orders of her family in a so-called honor killing.

Deeyah is also the recipient of several awards for her work supporting freedom of expression, and in 2012 she was awarded the Ossietzky prize by Norwegian PEN. The focus of her work and her access to voices that are often overlooked and misunderstood has led to an increasing demand for her to be a speaker at international human rights events and platforms, including the United Nations.

Deeyah is the founder and CEO of social purpose production company Fuuse, which creates works in the intersection of art and activism.

www.deeyah.com

YARROW KRANER

Yarrow Kraner is a professional director, photographer, and entrepreneur, who is a living example of the power of transformation. After graduating from film school, Yarrow moved to Los Angeles to direct commercials and music videos, and his creative ideas and work have been recognized all over the world.

Yarrow created Superdudes, called by *Wired* magazine "one of the pioneer social networking communities," which with 1.5 million subscribers by 1999 was the world's largest online game that also rewarded local community volunteerism. Involving celebrities, national charities, children's hospitals, and schools, it empowered young people to achieve their potential with the motto: "How do you save the world? Start with where you are . . ."

Yarrow's current projects include HATCH Experience, a non-profit organization formed to foster creativity through mentor-ship, exposure, and networking between filmmakers, musicians, photographers, designers, architects, writers, fine artists, acclaimed veterans in the entertainment industry, and others. "Designed to activate creativity to HATCH a better world," HATCH is a unique community movement that brings together and supports innova-tive thinkers and inventors across a range of disciplines. HATCH has connected over five hundred mentors to over five thousand stu-dents since 2004; HATCHexperience.org has been visited by people in over 150 countries, and some of the HATCH panels have been downloaded over a million times.

As well as directing projects for many leading companies, Yarrow has been recognized as a 2013 Aspen Institute Fellow and serves on the steering committee of Project Peace on Earth.

Yarrow's journey through life has led him to create projects that help to make the world a better place. In his words: "The inspiration of one can impact the lives of millions. Who's next?"

www.hatchexperience.org

DANIELE FINZI PASCA

Director, author, choreographer, and lighting designer, Daniele Finzi Pasca was born in Lugano in Switzerland. He grew up in a family of photographers and while young was introduced to the world of the circus. After serving the sick and dying in India, he returned to Switzerland and, with Maria Bonzanigo and his brother Marco, he founded the company Teatro Sunil to develop his "Theatre of Caress" vision of clowning, dance, and acting. Daniele has created and directed some twenty shows with Teatro Sunil which have been performed internationally, all of his creations being marked by a profound sense of humanity and playfulness.

For Cirque Éloize, cofounded with his wife Julie Hamelin Finzi, Daniele created *Nomade—At Night, the Sky is Endless* (2002) and *Rain—Comme une pluie dans tes yeux* (2003), for which he was nominated Best Director in New York's Drama Desk Awards. He wrote and directed Cirque du Soleil's *Corteo*, seen by over three million spectators. Daniele created and directed the closing ceremony of the Torino 2006 XX Winter Olympic Games, and in 2008 he was awarded the Swiss Theatre Prize and was nominated for the XIII Europe Theatre Prize. There followed *Donka—A Letter to Chekhov*.

Daniele has directed a number of operas in St. Petersburg, Naples, and elsewhere, and in 2011, he cofounded Compagnia Finzi Pasca, uniting his existing companies. In 2012, he was awarded the Hans Reinhart Ring, the highest distinction in Swiss theatre, for his lifelong contribution to the performing arts, and he composed *La Verità*, a new show that toured worldwide. In 2014 Daniele created and directed the Olympic Closing Ceremony and the Opening Ceremony of the Paralympics in Sochi, Russia.

Meanwhile, Daniele is still performing his solo show *Ícaro* all around the world. Other projects are in the making, including a movie, *Piazza San Michele*, a new theatrical clown show, and creating and directing the 2019 Winegrowers' Festival in Vevey, Switzerland, a unique four-times-a-century event that attracts hundreds of thousands.

www.finzipasca.com

ACKNOWLEDGMENTS

All of us at *Talent for Humanity* would like to thank the many individuals who took part in making this book possible.

First of all, our gratitude goes to the seven individuals whose lives and achievements have been featured in this book: Reza, Sherry and Bob Jason, Aliza Hava, Deeyah Khan, Yarrow Kraner, and Daniele Finzi Pasca. Each of them recounted their stories, which were then written by a number of talented writers. Reza's story was written by Rachel Deghati. The stories of Sherry and Bob, Aliza, and Yarrow were set down by Nadine Taylor and Barry Fox. Deeyah's story was told by Nicola Rowe and Joanne Payton. Daniele's story was written by Facundo Ponce de León. Thanks to Osanna Vaughn and Maya Bernardes for translation. We are also very grateful to Andrew Rich and Lorraine Velez, who did a lot of priceless editing work on the book. A special thanks to Kathryn Baker, Dennis Rodriguez, Guillame Sanchez, Célicia Theys and Kathy Barrett. Our gratitude goes as well to Simon Xavier Guerrand-Hermès, Daniel Magnus Cheifetz, Patrice Bilodeau, and Mario Luraschi for their contribution to this project.

All our thanks go to the supporters of *Talent for Humanity*, and especially to our executive team, and to members of the four circles: the Ethic & Development Circle, the Creative & Celebration Circle, the Young Talents Circle, and our Community Circle.

The overall editing of this book was managed by Patrick Gaffney, who also did some translations from French and wrote the introduction and final chapter of the book. He would like to claim complete responsibility for any mistakes, omissions, or excesses.

The aim of this book has been to share these remarkable accounts and to hearten and inspire human beings to reach out to others and find creative ways of helping humanity in whatever ways they can. One way to begin is by writing a *Letter to Humanity* and sending it through our website; another is to join our Community Circle. Please look at our website, where you can also read our Ethical Charter:

www.talentforhumanity.org

The subjects of this book are all recipients of the *Human Spirit Award*. *Talent for Humanity* is committed to donating proceeds from the sale of this book to the work of each of the seven individuals featured here.

NOTES

1 Frans de Waal, *Our Inner Ape* (New York: Penguin, 2005), p. 175.

2 Sogyal Rinpoche, *The Tibetan Book of Living & Dying*, rev. ed. (San Francisco: Harper, 2002), p. 191.

3 Piero Ferrucci, *The Power of Kindness* (New York: Penguin, 2006), p. 274.

4 Viktor E. Frankl, *Man's Search for Meaning* (Boston: Beacon Press, 2006), p. 133.

5 Shirley du Boulay, "Cicely Saunders: The Founder of the Modern Hospice Movement," *Daily Telegraph*, September 5, 2002.

6 Gary Ho, *The Life and Teachings of Venerable Master Cheng Yen* (Vancouver: Douglas and McIntyre, 2010), p.14.

7 Wangari Maathai, Nobel Peace Prize Lecture, Oslo City Hall, Oslo, Norway, December 10, 2004.

8 Murphy, Brian K, *Transforming Ourselves, Transforming the World* (Halifax, Fernwood, 1999), p.136.

9 Abuelaish, Izzeldin, *I Shall Not Hate* (New York: Walker, 2012), p.232.

10 Thich Nhat Hanh, *The World We Have* (Berkeley: Parallax, 2008), p.69.

11 Dalai Lama, "Live Life with Compassion," August 31, 2011, http://www.youtube.com/watch?v=SC-kwVyNNxw.

12 Ladinsky, Daniel, trans., *A Year with Hafiz* (New York: Penguin, 2011), p.397.

ABOUT TALENT FOR HUMANITY

Talent for Humanity recognizes, celebrates, and supports individuals whose talents had, and still have, a positive impact on humanity and serve as a source of inspiration to others. They are living examples of the capacity of each human being to transform the world.

Talent for Humanity is a young, international nonprofit organization conceived by a group of people drawn together by a single vision of serving humanity and by the idea that it is possible to create a better world through entertainment and the performing arts.

Talent for Humanity is a place where the art of inventing a world without frontiers is continuously encouraged, and imagination, creation, and talent are nurtured. We believe that we can fulfill our dreams without any limits

Talent for Humanity is organized around four Circles, whose aim is to discover and facilitate the contribution of talented and creative people to our projects. If you believe that you can bring something special to one of these Circles, do not hesitate to contact us at circles@talentforhumanity.org.

The Ethic & Development Circle is to ensure that we respect our engagement and commitment to serve humanity with open hearts and minds, as well as help the organization grow in a meaningful way.

The Creative & Celebration Circle is to develop and produce cultural projects around our themes with the aim of raising awareness and inspiring and encouraging others to initiate similar activities. The Circle serves to put values of the human spirit into practice and highlight such values through programs and entertainment events so as to increase their impact and make them accessible to a larger public.

The Young Talents Circle is open to anyone between the ages of sixteen and twenty-nine who desires to make a positive contribution to our society and believes that by transforming ourselves we can help transform the world. One of the first objectives of this Circle is to organize exhibits and conference events based on our different themes in universities, fine art schools, etc. The goal of the Young Talents Circle is to propose positive initiatives for our common future.

The Community Circle is a place where you can introduce yourself, submit your comments in support of our mission, and connect with similarly minded people.

If you believe that each and every one of us can achieve something by using our talent, whatever it may be, to help make this world the place we dream to live in, then join us.

talentforhumanity.org